HOW TO LIVE WELL

HOW TO LIVE WELL

Secrets of Using Neurosis

Takehisa Kora

Foreword by
David K. Reynolds

Translated by
Gregory Peterson
and
David K. Reynolds

STATE UNIVERSITY OF NEW YORK PRESS

This book was originally published as *Dô Ikiru Ka?*, Hakuyosha Publishers, Tokyo, 1979.

Production by Ruth Fisher
Marketing by Bernadette LaManna

Published by
State University of New York Press, Albany

© 1995 State University of New York

For information, address the State University of New York Press,
State University Plaza, Albany, NY 12246

Library of Congress Cataloging-in-Publication Data

Kōra, Takehisa, 1899–
    [Dō ikiru ka. English]
    How to live well : secrets of using neurosis / Takehisa Kora :
    foreword by David K. Reynolds ; translated by Gregory Peterson and
    David K. Reynolds.
        p.   cm.
    Includes index.
    ISBN 0-7914-2401-4 (cloth). — ISBN 0-7914-2402-2 (pbk.)
    1. Morita psychotherapy.   2. Conduct of life.   3. Neuroses.
I. Peterson, Gregory.   II. Reynolds, David K.   III. Title.
RC489.M65K6613   1995
616.89'14—dc20   94-18942
                                                                CIP

10 9 8 7 6 5 4 3 2 1

Contents

Foreword

This book was written by the senior Morita therapist in Japan. Dr. Takehisa Kora was Morita Masatake's student and successor to the Professorship of Psychiatry and Neurology at Jikei University School of Medicine in Tokyo. Emeritus Professor Kora is now in his mid-nineties and still active in the affairs of Morita therapy. His small hospital, Kora Koseiin, is well-known for its long history of inpatient Moritist practice.

I suggest that Kora's book be read as a source of experienced, grandfatherly advice notwithstanding its scholarly merits. It offers a flavor of the sometimes dogmatic, yet experienced-based, realistic attitude of senior Japanese medical men in this field.

Much of the material comes from Kora's Thursday lectures for patients and staff at Koseiin. I used to sit with them twenty-five years ago, understanding little because of my inability in Japanese in those days, soaking up the atmosphere of serious truths about the human condition mixed with occasional humor for release and perspective. Human wisdom doesn't change over the years despite advances in intellectual knowledge.

When Kora uses the word "neurosis" in this volume he is writing of what the Japanese call "shinkeishitsu" neurosis. Pure shinkeishitsu neurotics are not seen so often these days in Japan. Most patients bring a mixture of shinkeishitsu tendencies and depression or some other combination of symptoms. To some degree, however, we all share some of the shinkeishitsu traits described in this book. So Kora's writing is worth reading for its personal value as well as for its academic medical content.

Shinkeishitsu neurotic traits include tendencies toward introversion, over-cautiousness, self criticism, self analysis, perfectionism, idealism, high intelligence, sensitivity, asociality but not antisociality, worrying, persistence, and a desire for self improvement. Moritist theory holds that shinkeishitsu people have normal psychological processes that have been carried to extremes or misused because of mistaken ideas about the human condition. Shinkeishitsu people mistakenly believe that anxiety and fear shouldn't exist, that they can be controlled somehow by the will. Shinkeishitsu people mistakenly believe that they must always act from a base of self-confidence and inner calm. Such misconceptions about the reality of human life are corrected through the re-education provided by Morita's therapy. The patient is taught not only by means of lectures of the sort provided in this book but also by experiential assignments and feedback from everyday life.

In the West we have borrowed and extended the ideas from Morita Therapy and another Japanese therapy called Naikan to form what is called Constructive Living (Reynolds, 1976–1993). Kora's book provides Constructive Living (CL) instructors and others interested in CL practice with a historical reference point for considering our intellectual roots. Constructive Living instructors and students will find much that is familiar uniquely presented here in the style of a respected Japanese scholar-clinician.

The cultural approach championed in the West has usually emphasized the control of Nature. We have succeeded using science and technology to subdue some of Nature, use it to solve some of our current problems, and to meet some of our immediate needs. Such an approach doesn't work so well with problems of the mind. The East, with its emphasis on the acceptance and integration with Nature, *does* have something worth considering in matters of the mind. To consider that thoughts and feelings are natural phenomena, that they need not be resisted or conquered, and that they can be accepted like sunshine and thunderstorms may come as a novel perspective to many Westerners.

The fact of the matter is that the mind keeps changing; it is not fixed. So it is difficult to apply static diagnostic categories to it. It is difficult to treat elements of the mind and symptoms as though they were things that could be repaired. More than difficult, it may be meaningless. Please consider these dynamic Moritist ideas as the wind blows outside your room and the water flows into your sink and the fire in your gas pilot light flickers.

Dr. Masatake (or Shoma) Morita (1874–1938) was a psychiatrist and, I would argue, a philosopher of the early twentieth century. His contribution to psychiatric medicine is well-recognized in Japan. With the popularity of psychodynamic and behavioral therapies in Japan, however, the current practice of Morita Therapy in that country is limited but growing again, now that interest has picked up in the West and in China. The future of this realistic approach to living called Morita Therapy is bright.

David K. Reynolds, Ph.D.
Coos Bay, Oregon

Preface

There are many types of people in this world: heroes and cowards, saints and sinners, the wise and the foolish, geniuses and imbeciles, model citizens and misfits, the great and the small. I cannot help thinking of one very important type: ordinary people. In any case, ordinary people are the majority in this world. They are the standard, so we can say that they are ordinary. The structure of human society is made by these ordinary people; they are perhaps the ones whose power maintains its stability.

If there were too many heroes, we would have a world continually at war. A world of saints, however difficult to imagine, would be boring and humorless. It is said that Carlyle's wife grieved over having a genius for a husband. Many geniuses are eccentric or strange; some are not fit to be married.

We ordinary people have an infinite variety of personalities, but we have one thing in common: we can become capable, full-fledged members of society as long as we continue to work constructively, even if we are not born with superior abilities. In some cases we can be much better than average, or, on the other hand, we can be much worse than average.

I myself am a mediocre and ordinary person, so I understand ordinary people better than heroes or geniuses. Mediocre people have a variety of desires. Some want money, position, and fame; some want to have peaceful families; some want to be useful to society by doing good work. They want to love nature; have time to enjoy different interests and hobbies; pursue learning and wisdom; deepen their understanding of the arts; and, if possible, they want to demonstrate their abilities in their fields. We can say that the wish to build good character may be common to anybody.

Thus, mediocre people are somewhat acquisitive. They have difficulties because they don't have the abilities that are necessary to acquire everything they want. If they needed only money, or only power, or only learning, then things could be easier. However, they cannot be so eccentric, so they have many dilemmas. They tend to get mired in their sense of duty and compassion, and since their hearts are not as hard as iron, they go this way and that every time they meet difficulty. That is the way of ordinary human beings.

Ordinary people get entangled in many dilemmas in life and sometimes cannot demonstrate even half of their capability. When things go wrong, they pay too much attention to their own worries and weaknesses, even when they are objectively insignificant. Thus, they become obsessed by something, and the more they want to eliminate it, the more they become attached to it. Eventually they lose their freedom.

Neurotics are people who are in such neurotic states. They have such symptoms as irrational fears of relationships with others or of illness, depending on what obsesses them. There are other symptoms, such as morbid fears of being unclean, anxiety neuroses, insomnia, inferiority complexes, feelings of being heavy-headed, and so on. Although there are various symptoms, the root cause is the same.

Dr. Shoma Morita made it clear that such symptoms result from mental processes. A radical form of psychotherapy, Morita Therapy, was devised to treat neurotics by correcting their misconceptions of human nature, and by making them practice the right attitude toward daily life without depending on medication or rest.

Dr. Morita himself experienced neurotic symptoms in his youth; that is, he was also an ordinary man who tended to become obsessed. However, he discovered the fundamental nature of neurosis, or *shinkeishitsu*, and succeeded in developing a cure based upon his knowledge of psychiatry, his own experiences, and his observations while living with his patients. Thus Dr. Morita, though coming from an average standard, built a character that we consider expert, and we can see his constant striving, even while he suffered from illness. He was full of human kindness and continued his efforts to improve himself. He suffered and sorrowed in times of misfortune, but he was never overwhelmed. He had a wonderful sense of humor. He was a common, ordinary man who became great.

I learned from Dr. Morita and succeeded him. My main work for more than forty years has been the treatment and study of neurotics [*shinkeishitsusha*]. In my youth I suffered from neurotic symptoms, and so I have a sense of affinity with neurotic patients. Fortunately, with Morita Therapy, it has worked positively. I am a natural worrier with various desires and a hard worker with high aspirations, which is common among neurotic patients. The only difference is that the patients are suffering from their symptoms at present, while I am a counselor who is trying to help them become free.

This book summarizes what I actually *say* to the patients as a counselor, so there may be some poor writing; however, its frankness and vividness without reservation may be a merit. I will be pleased if this book is helpful, not only to patients who are suffering from neurotic symptoms, but also to anyone who has neurotic tendencies.

As I just mentioned, this book is based on notes from my talks. The original talks were all directed toward the same neurotics, so there is considerable repetition. I appreciate the Hakuyosha editorial staff for all of the trouble they took to make the talks into a book.

Takehisa Kora
Kora Koseiin Hospital, Tokyo

Part 1

Views of Life

1

Knowing Yourself

An ancient Greek philosopher said, "Know yourself," and I believe this is important in any age for personal growth in everyday life. I have been serving in mental health work for many years, and have treated many different people with neuroses and abnormal personalities who have recovered and returned to society. From long years of experience with such people I deeply believe that their personalities and their attitudes toward life would not have been distorted if they had truly known and accepted themselves as they actually were—if they had followed the way of *arugamama*, accepting reality as it is.

Self-Awareness and the Development of Character

What does it mean to know oneself? What is the proper way of *arugamama*? Personal development depends upon the depth of one's self-awareness. Everyone has good and bad qualities, and anyone who looks at himself deeply and honestly knows that he is not perfect. Although it may be unpleasant, we cannot deny that we sometimes have

3

unattractive feelings. Let us take jealousy as an example. This antisocial feeling, which may lead us to hurt others, is a manifestation of a desire for superiority and complete possession. People without jealousy are probably quite rare. Even a great, talented man like Goethe confessed his jealousy when Schiller won literary fame. There is jealousy not only in relationships between men and women, but also among friends and colleagues. It exists throughout society.

Some people are not deeply aware of their own jealousy. These people speak ill of others, delight in their failures and misfortunes and actively criticize them. Of course, I am not talking about constructive criticism. I am talking about those who try to raise their own worth by diminishing the worth of others. They do not realize that such actions come from their *own* jealousy. If they were more fully aware of the jealousy inside themselves, they would be ashamed to express it openly by speaking ill of others. They would naturally control their ugly gossip, and we could then call their personalities well-developed.

Soseki Natsume (author, 1867–1916) wrote in one of his novels that human beings are frightening because they can become evil instantly, even if they are usually good. When times are uneventful, the social side of human character emerges, but under certain conditions an antisocial side appears suddenly. For example, a politician, ordinarily a good man, may try to buy votes in an election campaign. If one is always aware of the fact that he, too, has an antisocial side, then he may be alert enough to protect himself from evil in a crisis.

Correct Self-Evaluation

People who cannot admit and accept their weaknesses, who believe they are always right, are insufferable. (Of course, some people suffer from delusions of grandeur, but we shall not consider such serious mental illnesses here.) People who have strong feelings of superiority overvalue themselves. When they have little ability, they become chronic complainers who blame others when things go wrong. We can see this tendency among self-righteous people who claim that morality and justice are on their side.

On the other hand, there are some people, including many neurotics, who suffer from inferiority complexes. They are not antisocial, and it is a pity that they cannot apply their full capabilities. Their feelings of inferiority focus on various shortcomings of appearance, physique, health, family environment, wealth, ability, or personality. Although such matters are of little importance objectively, such people have lost confidence because of their strong desires for perfection. Everyone who has a desire for improvement has some feeling of inferiority that can stimulate him to work harder, so we can say that such feelings are even useful. When one becomes boastful, his progress stops.

Hideyo Noguchi (microbiologist, 1876–1927) was born into an extremely poor family, and a serious burn crippled his hand at an early age. His handicap stimulated his fighting spirit, and he went on to become a great scientist. Demosthenes in ancient Greece (384–322 BC) was a stutterer, but it is said that he became an eloquent speaker by training himself. Thus, feelings of inferiority can lead to constructive change. Some people, however, become negative and believe that their inferiority makes them *incapable* of doing anything, and so they become unable to exercise their abilities fully. These people are not really inferior, but they are enslaved by inferiority complexes because of their unrealistically negative self-images. I consider these people a great loss to society.

Inferiority Complexes and Neurosis

Neurotics most accurately epitomize people who cannot accept themselves as they really are. These people feel sorry for themselves and anxiously monitor themselves and their abilities. For example, when I test those who complain of poor memory or concentration, I cannot find them objectively inferior in any way. Some complain that they tend to get tired easily, but experiments prove otherwise. Brain wave tests demonstrate that people who complain of insomnia often get much more sleep than they realize or admit. That is why I consider their symptoms less than what they claim. They tend to judge themselves with anxious feelings of inferiority, and, therefore, they do not really know themselves.

However, these people, even with their inferiority complexes, can be freed from their suffering by developing more accurate self-images and more self-confidence through the experience of success. The experiential treatment of neurosis works in this way. Accurate self-awareness means knowing one's true self and knowing that one's experiences are not necessarily unique, that is, the knowledge that something that makes one happy can make others happy, and something difficult for one can be difficult for others as well. Such a view of human equality produces empathy and bonds of solidarity with other people.

Obsessive desires for perfection come from a lack of self knowledge and, thus, inadequate knowledge of human nature. By ignoring the known facts of human nature, these people are always disappointed by their unrealistic desires. For example, a person who is obsessed with the desire for perfect feelings tries to feel refreshed at all times. In fact, however, our daily feelings naturally flow and change according to internal and external conditions, like the weather. A person who insists upon feeling refreshed is like one who hopes to have clear sky all the time; as soon as he sees a bit of a cloud, he assumes the weather will be terrible all day. When he feels just a little out of sorts, he tells himself that he is no good, and he makes himself feel worse.

Not Perfectionism, but Psychological Reality

Perfectionists are obsessed with the way they think they should be, ignoring themselves as they really are. They demand conditions in accord with their unrealistic ideals for themselves, which results in lost confidence since reality always works against them.

A student was suffering from the inability to read because of distracting thoughts when he tried to study. His suffering was caused by his belief that a reader should concentrate only on his book, that unrelated thoughts should not occur. Like this student, if one tries to eliminate digressive thoughts because they are in the way, then the opposite effect is achieved: one becomes more aware of them. Again he tries to get rid of them, getting into a vicious cycle, and then he cannot read at all. This student was attempting the impossible ideal of not having any distracting thoughts, fighting against each thought that entered his mind.

When one is reading, there is a natural rhythm of tension and relaxation, and when one is relaxed various thoughts occur naturally. One should accept this inevitable fact flexibly and continue to read on and off in rhythm. Thus, when distracting thoughts come to mind, one is not particularly conscious of them, so they do not interfere. It is important for people to recognize such psychological realities and to avoid struggling against them.

Under the Present Conditions

Our mental and physical states continually change. A person who knows himself recognizes this, and regardless of whether his condition is good or bad, he tries to do whatever he can. A normal person's attitude is to do seventy or eighty percent of something as well as possible when he cannot do one hundred percent of it perfectly. Perfectionists, however, ignore their real selves and cling to the best they have ever accomplished, expecting to be in top condition all the time. Their best performances are rare, so they are always dissatisfied with the present, and they exaggerate the importance of their minor shortcomings, which worsens their condition. In some serious cases their attitudes toward themselves prevent them from doing anything at all unless they are in peak condition. These people are true neurotics.

We all have various mental and physical shortcomings. We can never be satisfied if we look at ourselves only by the demanding standards of our ideals. Some people try to escape from reality by making excuses for their weaknesses, and some people do great work even with serious handicaps. The best example would be Helen Keller, who had three serious physical handicaps.

It is important to recognize that we tend to make all kinds of excuses in order to avoid suffering. For example, one may escape from attending a meeting by saying he has a slight cold. He feels guilty just skipping it for no reason, so he uses a minor illness as his excuse. This is an escape into illness. On the other hand, when he goes fishing, his attitude is reversed: he thinks his cold will disappear when he gets to the sea. If one gets into the habit of using illness as an excuse, then he becomes a neurotic.

Knowing Your Feelings

An important part of understanding one's self is knowing the nature of human emotions. First, we must admit that when the waves of our emotions rise in response to stimulation, it is impossible to restore tranquility by reason. Even if one wishes to be released quickly from negative feelings caused by an unpleasant incident, he cannot control them by willpower. Everyone experiences this kind of thing. Thus, there is a side over which we have no control, and there is a side where we have relatively wide room to use our free will as human beings.

Emotional matters are very often beyond our control. The adjustment of a train fare can be done on the spot, but emotional matters are hard to adjust immediately. For example, when someone with an average income loses one thousand yen, it is not such a serious matter for him. He feels bad, but that feeling does not stay too long. If it is ten thousand yen, the bad feeling stays a little longer. If it is one hundred thousand yen, it stays even longer. If he loses one million yen, then he will feel depressed for quite a long time. Even if he tells himself that he can do nothing about his loss, which is true, his feelings cannot be adjusted right away.

Although matters of reason and logic can be modified very easily, emotional matters are very often hard to adjust. However, some people are too eager to eliminate these unpleasant feelings right away. They do not understand the nature of emotions. Trying to do the impossible complicates matters by disturbing a natural process and, as a result, negative emotions stay longer. Moreover, such people suffer from being too slow in giving up their negative emotions.

The most important characteristic of emotions is that strong feelings subside with the passage of time if they are *left to run their course.* Our lives would be destroyed by suffering were it not for this phenomenon. For example, if the pain of a hard blow, such as the death of one's child, remained as strong as in the beginning, then no one could survive the endless pain. In fact, however, the waves of emotion rise and fall, gradually tapering off, whether we like it or not. When emotions begin to take over in labor-management disputes, negotiators sometimes take advantage of this principle by declaring cooling-off periods.

The fact that emotions fade is a great blessing, but sometimes it has a negative effect, recognized in such Japanese expressions as "a nine day wonder." For example, when people decide to quit smoking or drinking after being deeply moved by some experience, some cannot persist because their powerful emotions fade away as time passes.

Some people either ignore or do not know this principle of emotions, and they become desperate when they encounter trouble, as if it would last forever. They cannot trust the passage of time. An expert in living knows that, however terrible his experience may be, his unpleasant feelings will fade with time, and so he can live with optimism.

Outer Self and Inner Self

How do people change? How can one change himself into a better person? In ancient Buddhist terms, "When the outer facet is tidied up, the inner facet will naturally follow." The outer facet is one's external behavior, and the inner facet is one's mental and emotional side. When one lowers his head in front of a statue of Buddha with his hands pressed together, then spontaneously he begins to feel reverent. If he throws his head back haughtily, reverent feelings do not emerge. We can conclude that, regardless of the mind, if one first tries to straighten himself externally, then his spirit changes to fit the outside reality.

When I treat neurotics, I advise them to improve their form. That makes it much easier to practice. We know that our athletic spirit awakens when we put on sportswear and sports shoes. This does not happen when one stands with his hands in the pockets of his trousers. When we frown, with our jaws clamped together and our fists tight, it is impossible to relax. When we smile, our tempers subside, and when we frown, we become bad-tempered. External form changes internal moods.

External form includes behavior. It is hard to change feelings only by thoughts or intentions; they change as a result of actions. For example, if I am in a sluggish mood, it is just about impossible to make myself feel invigorated as I am. But if I take off my jacket, climb up into a tree in the garden, and start cutting withered branches, then my feelings are energized by my activity. On a cold morning it is hard to get out of bed, so if you are going to get up only after your desire to get up matures, you will sleep all day. However, once you jump out of bed, your mood follows your action and changes completely. That is why no one goes back to bed again once he gets up.

If one is going to study only after his desire matures, then he will find it difficult to begin. He should first just sit at his desk, open an appropriate book, and start reading. The rhythm of studying is carried by the activity. First, make the form without waiting for the mood. Leave your feelings as they are and proceed with action first, and then it is easy and practical to change your state of mind. You need to recognize and practice such psychological realities in order to change yourself more constructively.

Anxiety and Pain

I have used the term *arugamama* already, but I would like to explain more about it. First, we have to recognize the fact that we humans are born with anxiety and pain and that these are necessary for our survival. Although it would seem better not to feel pain simply because we do not like it, the sense of pain alerts us to illness or injury where it hurts, and so it provides a natural mechanism to protect ourselves from external injuries.

Anxiety, another distasteful feeling, is the same. People are not the center of nature. Disasters happen every year, and we are surrounded by hostile microbes that continually multiply. Also, although human society was created by humans, it is not made for individuals; so if one does not make some effort, he will drop out since competition is very keen. There are numerous threats, such as illnesses, accidents, poor human relations, and economic problems. We have to admit that anxiety about such dangers is part of human life. We make constructive efforts only when we are motivated by such basic anxiety.

Life stagnates and deteriorates without anxiety and pain. In sports, the anxiety that one may be defeated by the opponent builds tension that makes us practice hard. Illness frightens us, so we observe the rules of health. If we did not have fear, we would not be able to avoid sudden dangers, such as an oncoming car. However, since a person who is obsessed by a desire for perfection does not *admit the necessity and the inevitability of these basic fears,* he wishes to avoid any kind of anxiety and pain. His wish that such anxiety and pain should not exist does not match reality. This kind of selfish desire is deceptive: as one becomes more acutely conscious of anxiety and pain, he may be obsessed by it. This is also a mistake which comes from not knowing one's *arugamama* self: the real self in the real world.

A key element of *arugamama* is to accept our inevitable physical or psychological reactions as they are, not to deny or resist the reaction, nor to stumble through by self-deception. For example, people get frightened when they climb to high places. They get nervous in front of large audiences. Their thoughts wander when they study. They cannot sleep when they have something to worry about. We all feel sluggish or weary or inferior sometimes.

Arugamama means knowing that such mind-body phenomena are inevitable and accepting them as they are. It is important to recognize this *arugamama* self with humility.

If, on the contrary, one tries to rid himself of such a weakness because it inconveniences him, then instead he becomes more acutely aware of it, and he will end up more troubled than before. For example, a neurotic who suffers from insomnia cannot sleep because of the ticking of a clock, and so he gets up and stops the clock. His attention stays with the sound because he treats it as a nuisance and tries to get rid of it. Ordinary people do not resist the sound as it is. Left to its nature, human attention does not remain focused on one thing. It moves away without notice, so ordinarily one does not continue to hear the sound of a clock even if it is still there.

Arugamama: Fulfilling the Desire to Improve

Arugamama concerns the question of how to accept sensory data from events or objects, even when we fear such stimuli. The first time anyone tries to jump into a pool from a high diving board, anxiety attacks him. This is natural. So, if one rejects his fear and decides to dive only after conquering it, he will never be able to take the first leap. Trying to overcome such inevitable fear through mental activity is impossible, and the more one tries, the more strongly one becomes conscious of it. This is not *arugamama*; it is an unnatural willfulness. Do not confuse *arugamama* with *akirame* [surrender, giving up].

Akirame means to avoid jumping in because of fear. *Arugamama* means to jump in anyway, fear and all. To jump in only after conquering fear is willful and unnatural.

Moreover, *arugamama* includes the fact that everyone is born with a strong desire to improve and develop. To get on with is the attitude of *arugamama*, which distinguishes it from *akirame*. When one tries to dive into a pool, the natural fear is as it is: *arugamama*. Accepting that fear as a fact and yet diving in, heeding the will to grow, is true *arugamama*, unlike the negativity *akirame*. Likewise, when one tries to speak in front of a large group of people, if he accepts his nervousness with the attitude of *arugamama*, and, knowing he is tense, speaks without running away, soon his mind begins to concentrate on the speech, and eventually his nervousness simply fades away. Even if this inevitable psychological process is distasteful, I believe that it is natural and fruitful to accept it and to continue to try to fulfill the desire for self-development.

I have discussed the confusion that results from not knowing oneself and the constructive meaning of accurate self-knowledge. I would like next to mention one more important point: I would like you to consider what your real wishes are. Most people can discover that their true desires are to use their abilities fully and to work for the benefit of themselves and others.

If you recognize that you have a desire for improvement and development, then you will need to keep working according to your real wishes, even when you have to endure hard times. If your real wish is the desire to grow, your whole life will naturally deteriorate if your way of living does not go along with this desire. If one is happily dependent on someone else and lives a lazy and unproductive life, then he does not have the desire for improvement, so nothing can be done. As Confucius said, "Rotten wood cannot be carved." If you recognize the desire for improvement in yourself, then there is no other way than to try to make it happen.

2

Reality Is the Only Truth

Obeying Human Nature

Dr. Morita always emphasized that reality is the only truth. It is important to recognize the facts honestly and to act according to reality. This is particularly important for neurotics because neurotic people tend to be controlled by their emotions. They interpret events with their own feelings, not recognizing the facts as they are (*arugamama*). They tend to respond to their ideas of what should be instead of what is, increasing their mental contradictions.

For example, concerning human relations, one can meet some people without any problems, some people in a reserved manner, and in front of some people one feels a lot of pressure. An outpatient said he felt great pressure from two of his colleagues in particular, and he could not do anything about it. When he was a student, he had the same kind of strong feelings about certain groups of classmates. At any rate, everyone has some fear of certain people, but those with neurotic anxieties about human relations have a tendency to believe "I should be calm. I should be at ease in any situation."

This is not realistic. Our feelings change every time we meet someone. One feels anxious before a large audience, and feels stiff and nervous in front of someone whose favor he seeks: as an ordinary company man becomes nervous in front of his superiors. A variety of feelings is a common fact of human nature among ordinary people. To live with a clear recognition of the fact, to live according to reality, is *arugamama*. Dr. Morita said that neurotics who suffer from the fear of meeting others fight against the reality of human nature and try to ignore it.

Live According to Reality

When someone says he feels good or bad today he rarely knows the specific cause of his mood. That is the reality. Whether you feel good or bad, you do whatever you can, and that is the way to live according to reality. If one thinks he should feel refreshed all the time, then he will always be disappointed. One who often complains of heaviness in his head is like a person who thinks the sky should be clear all the time.

I would like to consider people who have a morbid fear of cancer. Such people anxiously wonder if they have cancer, or they are controlled by the feeling that they may develop cancer, and they are obsessed by such fears. However, the fact is that they do not have cancer no matter how much they check. That one does not have cancer is a fact, but he is controlled by the possibility of having cancer.

People who have a morbid fear of heart disease are always afraid of dying of heart failure. No matter how much they check, and regardless of the fact that there is no danger, they are controlled by their concern for the possibility that something might happen. This concern is not based on the facts.

Scientists base their work on facts; if they work by their feelings, then there is no science. Once a famous American neurologist, Baird, called the symptoms of what we now call neurosis, "neurasthenia." He considered it a result of weakened nerves, which resulted in patients being over-sensitive and easily fatigued. However, Dr. Morita did not accept such a theory; instead, he observed the facts and proved that neurosis is not caused by the weakening of nerves. He lived with his patients and found that they could live actively, bear quite heavy labor, and do mental work. For example, some patients passed their college entrance examinations while still hospitalized. All of these facts clearly proved that their bodies and minds were not debilitated. After all, it became clear that neurosis is not a matter of weak nerves, and so he rejected the term *shinkei suijaku* (neurasthenia) as the name of the disease.

A new neurology was born from the observation of facts. The symptoms of neurosis show a condition in which patients are often controlled by their feelings.

Living with Anxiety

Anxiety permeates life. That is a fact. Strictly speaking, there is no human condition without anxiety, so we might as well recognize that our fears will be with us as long as we live. Neither society nor nature is made to be convenient for us as individuals. Innumerable objects of anxiety exist: earthquakes, lightning, fires, illnesses, economic and human relations problems. Therefore, we should think that it is natural for us to have anxiety.

We live and work with anxiety, which actually has positive benefits. If there were no anxiety, we would not try at all. We study because we fear failure, and we keep ourselves healthy because we are afraid of illness. We make great efforts and struggle for success because we have the anxiety of failing in society. Our lives are stimulated by anxiety, so anxiety has a positive meaning. That is why if one wishes a life without anxiety, that person surely falls into internal discord. He always asks himself why he feels anxious.

We cannot count all the objects of our anxiety. One characteristic of a healthy person is that he may have many fears but he is not obsessed by any one of them. However, neurotics are abnormal in that they limit the problem to a particular object and suffer from it all the time. For example, one who abnormally fears human contact fixes his attention on his interpersonal relations, while one who suffers from an obsession with cleanliness fears only dirtiness. At any rate, it is important not to treat a specific fear in a special way and to take anxiety as natural. Therefore, *arugamama* means to accept such anxiety as it is, to recognize the facts as they are, and to keep making efforts according to our basic drives for improvement and development.

3

Phrases for Spiritual Training

Munen Muso (freedom from all ideas and thoughts)

Fudoshin (immobility of determination)

Hibi kore kojitsu (every day a good day)

Sanmaikyo (perfect spiritual concentration)

Ware and muga (self and selflessness)

In Japanese there are many phrases which, at first glance, seem very good for moral training. On the contrary, if you swallow these words uncritically, they sometimes cause trouble. If you take the meaning of the phrase *hibi kore kojitsu* as simply, "Every day should be a good day," then often things do not go the way you want. We have many good phrases, such as *hibi kore kojitsu*, and I would like to consider some of them here.

We hear that we should be *munen muso*, free from all ideas and thoughts, when we do things. The extreme state of *munen muso* is death, but also in a coma or deep sleep one's state could be called *munen muso*. In practice, since the

19

human brain works ceaselessly when one is awake, he always senses something, thinks, feels, and exercises his will. *Munen muso* is, therefore, a metaphor; it is, in other words, nothing but *sanmaikyo*.

Sanmaikyo is a condition that one and the object of his attention become one, that is, he "becomes the thing itself." In emergencies anyone can become that way under pressure. When a Sumo wrestler is asked how he did it after he knocked over a strong opponent, he answers that he does not know because he was beside himself. When he struggles hard, his mind is in an extremely active condition, and the object and himself become one, so there was no difference between subject and object.

By the way, a person with a pure heart can accept things as they are, so not only during emergencies but also in ordinary activities he can develop *sanmaikyo*. He can taste a cup of tea innocently and be happy with a smiling face of a child. When he sees a cloud he becomes a cloud, when he sees a flower he becomes a flower, when he sees a goldfish he becomes a goldfish.

Fudoshin (A Stable Mind)

The meaning of the word *fudoshin* can be taken as being calm in any situation, or not being influenced by feelings of sorrow or joy, and being self-controlled at all times. You may think anyone would want to achieve this state. However, if one has *fudoshin* literally, then what happens? When a car appears suddenly from the side during his walk, if he cannot be startled, then he cannot avoid the car instantly. If one is calm at the death of a loved one, then we should call him not one who has *fudoshin* but rather one who has no heart.

When I was in the prime of my life, I worked at a large mental hospital. Eighty percent of the patients were elderly schizophrenic patients. I was shocked to discover that they did not get surprised at earthquakes or fires, and that they were calm when a roommate hanged himself. Rather than a good meaning of *fudoshin*, this is apathy.

One characteristic of a healthy person is that his feelings change with every situation. If one has anxiety and pain, feelings of sorrow or of joy, and still takes the road of improvement with a daily constructive attitude, and if he can keep this attitude all his life no matter what happens, then that is a great example of *fudoshin*.

Ware and Muga: Self and Selflessness

Next there are expressions that mean "selflessness." During the war *messhi houkou* (self-annihilation for the sake of the nation) was enforced. This was often used by oppressors to sacrifice people, and it has no place in this discussion. On the other hand, we also have words with antisocial meanings, such as *gashitsu* (attachment to oneself), *ga wo haru* (to insist on one's own way), or other expressions that refer to selfishness or self-centeredness.

It is said that modern philosophy started at the discovery of the self, and we cannot deny the existence of *ware* (oneself). Even if we deny everything else, *ware* stays with us to the end. A literal meaning of *muga* (nonexistence of self) cannot exist in fact, so we should take the word as a metaphor to describe a state of action. The phrase, "to sacrifice personal interests for the public good," expresses a high ethic, and in unusual cases ordinary people reach this state. Generally, a person does not have selfishness when he jumps into a river water to save a drowning boy; however, we are not purely altruistic about what we do in our daily lives. People have an instinct for self-preservation. However, we can live in ways that allow us to serve others and, as a result, this will lead to self-improvement and development.

No one wants to work for a company that does not pay a salary. As ordinary people, our attitude is to work hard for an organization while, at the same time, our work leads to our own development. If one is too selfish, then he becomes antisocial, people avoid him, and he does not feel comfortable living there. But, on the other hand, if one tries to contribute and be useful in his present environment, then he feels more satisfied and comfortable. That is, if one lives to be useful to others, he realizes through his experience that his life means the expansion of himself.

Muga is sometimes used with the same meaning as *munen muso* or *mushin* (innocent). There is a metaphor to describe a good jockey riding a horse: "no man on the saddle, and no horse under the saddle," which means the man and the horse are one body. Another phrase, *butsuga ryoubou*, also means that a person becomes one with the object, the condition of being the thing itself.

If one starts struggling with *ware*, fighting with the internal self, then there is no limit. Patients who fear interpersonal encounters place importance on defending themselves, so they become very sensitive to what others think of them. *Tanin* (others) and *ware* (self) are opposed to each other, creating tension. The more one tries to get rid of *ware*, the more he becomes conscious of it. When one is going to have a face-to-face talk, and if he just tries to get on with the matter at hand, then he will naturally free himself from self-centeredness. If one can realize the attitude of being in touch with reality, then his fear of facing people, which sticks to a small self, will gradually disappear.

Hibi Kore Kojitsu (Every Day a Good Day)

Last, I would like to discuss *hibi kore kojitsu*. Everyone wants every day to be a good day, and many people welcome such phrases. However, if one wants to have the literal meaning of the phrase, then he is sure to get into a contradiction. Our health is not necessarily good all the time. According to external and internal conditions our moods naturally rise and fall, as can be said about the weather. Whatever one's circumstances, if the meaning of one's life is realized by working not for himself but for others, and if one is in poor physical or mental health, and does not hurt others in his misery, then his days are good days. There are some people who have serious illnesses and yet positively influence the people around them all the time; but there are others who, although they have objectively light handicaps, exaggerate their problems and afflict others. There, depending on one's attitude, a bad day could be a good day and even a wonderful day could be a bad day.

I often see plants in the garden around my clinic. Koseiin has enough plants to become designated a forest reserve of Shinjuku Ward. There are some very old trees, and there are many plants that I started myself. I am especially interested in the ones I planted; I have special memories of each plant, and when I am in the garden I feel that I am surrounded by my loved ones. The old man next door made shelves in his small garden for several dozen Azalea bonsai and takes good care of them every day. A person who has something he loves is a person who has good days. People naturally start feeling love toward whatever they have nurtured or kept for a long time, such as plants, animals, humans or personal belongings in everyday use. The life that is surrounded by cherished things or people is *hibi kore kojitsu*, a rich life filled with good days. There is an even more positive example of *hibi kore kojitsu*: a life in which one continues to do constructive work and sees or anticipates its development. A person with a creative attitude toward life can have many wonderful days, but a lazy person can have very few.

People can experience *hibi kore kojitsu* in a wide variety of ways: by actions, by appreciating nature or the arts, by satisfying intellectual curiosity, by loving. If a person can have many kinds of good days, then I would call that person wealthy.

4

Views of Life

Views of Life Change

There is no absolutely correct philosophy of life. It changes
with the times. During the time of prewar loyalty many
people placed great value on patriotism. They were taught
to believe that way by the people in power at the time.
Today few people have such a view of life. In the days of
the samurai, when those who had been wronged could
dispense justice themselves, revenge was considered a great
virtue. If you practice such revenge today, you are going to
get into very serious trouble.

One's view of life depends on the times and also on
one's age. That is why one's outlook at twenty years old is
what it is at the time, not something absolute. You do not
know when it will change, and so you cannot help but leave
the future as your future assignment. When you are in your
thirties, it changes; and in your fifties, sixties, and seventies,
it changes accordingly. At my age I have my outlook, but I
do not know how it will change when I become 100 years
old. (If I am still living at that age, I am afraid I might not
have a view of life since I might be senile!)

When one is a little child, he is not aware of his view of life, and his desire to sleep and eat precedes everything. This is the most important thing for a baby, who grows by sleeping: "Babies who sleep a lot grow a lot." When babies are not sleeping, they are eating. When they grow older, they become interested in the opposite sex, and they consider their interests important. When some Japanese women near the age of twenty, they place great importance on marriage, or they begin to show a great deal of concern about their appearance. They want to appear as attractive as possible, which is why they wear make-up. On the other hand, young Japanese men place more importance on their study, sports or love. In the prime of their lives they usually place importance on their work. There are many more views of life as people age.

Views of life depend on the people who hold them. Politicians generally have strong desires for power, and they control others with their desire. Extreme examples are people like Hitler, Napoleon or Nobunaga. Hitler was a slave to his morbid desire for power. He would do anything, no matter how cruel, to satisfy his desire, and that was his attitude toward life. That is why he was a large-scale criminal. Everyone has some desire for power, although not to such an extent.

Some people have very strong desires for material objects or for money. In extreme cases, there are some who are like usurers, who are interested in nothing but money matters, and who have no sense of duty or humanity. However, all ordinary people desire material possessions and money more or less. There may be differences of degree, but we would be lying if we refused to admit that we had such desires.

Some people have refined desires, such as the desire to pursue truth by studying, and some of them become scholars. There are some honorable people who want to do good for their society, and they place importance on living for the love of mankind, contributing to society.

Hypochondria

There are many people who place importance on health. If one places too much importance on it, he starts worrying too much, especially if anything goes wrong. If he focuses only on the state of his health, he becomes like a measuring instrument for himself. To place such extreme importance on one's physical condition is called hypochondria.

Generally speaking, ordinary people, myself included, do not place extreme importance on any one thing; instead, we value many things. If you think about yourself, then you would understand what I mean. You want to have as good a spouse as possible, you want to have a certain minimum salary, you want to be healthy; maybe you want to become great to a certain degree, or you want to have some power or fame. In this way you have various desires. Such are the desires of ordinary people.

When their desires are distorted, many people become eccentric. There are good eccentrics and bad ones. There are many whose sole desire is for learning. These people contribute to our knowledge and understanding, so they are valuable eccentrics. We cannot say they are bad just because they are different. Our attitudes toward life change according to what we consider important and, as a result, our views of life differ.

Reversed Myth

Views of life in Medieval Europe centered around God. They believed that God had created heaven and earth in a week. God's creation was earth-centered, and among the living things on the earth humans were at the center. Naturally they said the heavenly bodies went around the earth, and on the earth humans were the best. They said, "God created people in the image of God."

However, in modern days the theory of creation is completely reversed. This was caused first by developments in astronomy. As a result of these developments we now know that earth is not the center, that it is only a small planet that goes around a fixed star, the sun, among infinite numbers of heavenly bodies. There are about twenty billion stars in the Milky Way, our galactic system. The sun is but one of those stars. There are about 100 billion nebulae like the Milky Way. This is quite amazing, and some scholars imagine that there are more than 100 million planets that have the same conditions as the earth. If you look at humans from this point of view, we are really tiny. However, we can imagine such things, so we have some greatness.

The theory that people were made by God after His image, taught by Medieval theologians, was challenged by Darwin's theory of evolution, which was rapidly proved by fossil remains. Peking man was not an ape, but it looks too much like an ape to be called a human. Neanderthal man was human, but many remains of humans in lower stages of evolution have been excavated. From such stages in the series emerged modern human beings. Among the living things on earth humans are probably at the top of evolution because our nervous systems are especially advanced. However, the reason we think we are evolved from animals is that we have many animal characteristics. We can think of very noble things, but on the other hand we have the same instincts as the lower animals. The actions humans perform by nature can be very primitive.

That is why human beings have good points and bad points. We have social phases and antisocial phases, too. Old theatrical performances distinguish the heroes from the villains. Heroes do only good things, and villains do only bad things. In reality, however, such cases are very rare. "Villains" sometimes do good things.

Chuji Kunisada, a legendary Robinhood-like figure in epic tales of Japan, has a positive image because of his occasional good deeds in behalf of the weak, but he actually did many bad deeds. He was a gambler, a good-for-nothing. He was violent and troublesome. In the end he was crucified, but the *Koudan* and *Naniwa-bushi* tales exaggerated the rare good deeds he performed.

My discussion has gone off the track, but any bad man has some good facets, and any good man has antisocial aspects. Soseki Natsume wrote, "Usually a good man does bad things in a crisis, so one must be on guard," and when I read it I was impressed. This is a true story that caused a controversy in a foreign country: after a shipwreck there was no food, and the survivors ate human flesh. Of course, no one eats human flesh in ordinary circumstances, but people can do even that in a crisis.

Being Aware of Human Nature

If you are aware of what human beings can do in times of crisis, then you can become a well-developed person. A person who always believes that he is right is troublesome. If one thinks that whatever he does is right, then he tends to blame others when things go wrong. In Christianity a person who is obsessed with the idea that he is always right is called a Pharisee. A truly refined person does not think he is the only one who is right. If you examine yourself, then you would know it well. That is why it is necessary to understand human nature from different angles.

You may feel fear in front of other people. If you assume, "When I meet people, I have to be calm in any situation," or, "When I study, I should be able to concentrate without having any other thoughts in my mind," then that is a false idealism and an attitude of perfectionism. Reality itself does not cause such complications.

If you are well aware that your own condition varies like the weather, and that it is human nature to change, then you will not be enraptured when you are in good circumstances, and you will not need to be too pessimistic in adverse situations. You should recognize the fact that your circumstances are flowing and changing, and you should do whatever you can in the situation. Therefore, even if you have neurotic symptoms, it is important not to feel too easy in good circumstances or too pessimistic in times of adversity.

Part 2

Unpleasant but Necessary

5

Pitfalls of Neurosis

Exaggerating Minor Physical Disorders

When you feel a heaviness in your head, you naturally feel depressed. Although it has nothing to do with intelligence, everyone has similar tendencies, depending on the occasion, and your mental vitality is reduced in such circumstances. It is not good to think of this kind of condition as a sign of serious illness or to worry too much about it. If we compare this condition to that of a machine, we can say that the machine has some friction and needs some grease. On such an occasion you must trust that it is going to improve and you must wait for that time.

One's physical condition can be good or bad depending on the day. In my case, when I have a meeting until late, I feel tired the next day, but I do not consider it an illness. It is no good to think of illness whenever your physical condition is poor. Although it is within the limit of normal physiological change, if you pay anxious attention to it by thinking of it as illness, then, as if you are hypnotized, you start thinking about it more and more. It becomes a vicious cycle. Even if you feel some physical disorder or have some weak physical condition, you should strive to do what a healthy person would do.

The "Only I" Complex

Everyone feels afraid of other people sometimes. Recently I went to a university class reunion. Among the eleven people present, who were all about my age, a man sitting across from me is practicing medicine in Tokyo. He asked me, "Although I am okay when I am drinking, I tremble when I am not drinking. Am I an alcoholic?"

I said, "An alcoholic stops trembling when he drinks, and trembles when he does not drink, but in your case you tremble only in front of other people, right?"

He said, "Yes, I am practicing *nagauta* (long epic songs), but I decided not to attend a training meeting where I would have to sing in front of other people."

I asked, "Why?"

He said, "When I participate, I shorten my life," but, in short, he probably has a fear of other people. I see him often at meetings, but I have never noticed that he had any such anxiety. He also said that he could not write well in the presence of other people.

At the class reunion we were all comrades; so many interesting stories came out. One said, "Since I was young, I have been a poor talker. Even in front of women I like, I have never been able to express myself. Too bad."

I asked him, "At your age you are all right now, aren't you?"

He said, "Even now it is the same." He can live his everyday life normally, but in special circumstances he cannot do well unless he drinks. He has a house he is renting out, and he wants to raise the rent since he has not done so for many years. He cannot tell the tenant when he is sober, so he does so after drinking. When he drinks too much, he says too much and things do not go right, so he tries to moderate his drinking. If he keeps on, he will become an alcoholic.

He may think he has an abnormal fear of interpersonal contact, but no one can detect it. I found out only after he told me. However, a person who fears contact with others thinks everyone else knows it, so when his hands tremble a little, he is really ashamed and thinks that everyone is looking down on him. I do not pay special attention to my nervousness, so I do not care whether my hands tremble or not. He makes an important issue of it, so he gets nervous and his hands shake. If he could think the purpose of this meeting were to drink, he could drink even with his trembling, and then everything would be all right.

When you write, your purpose is to write legibly. As long as your writing suits its purpose it is fine, and so whether your hands tremble or not is related merely to the act of writing. If you get on with meeting your objectives, everything will surely work out to achieve your purpose. When you catch a ball, if you look at the ball, then it is okay; if you look at your hands, all the time worrying about how to use them, your attention strays away from the ball, and you will drop it. As long as you are looking at the ball, your hands move naturally to catch it without your conscious awareness of their movements.

When you pick up a cup, as long as you get on with the purpose of picking it up, then your hands move the shortest distance to grasp the handle. You are not aware of your movements one by one, but as long as you get on with the purpose, they will all harmonize. That is why you will be freed from self-centered obsessions naturally if you lead a reality-centered life and strive positively toward your goals.

Distorted Self-Defense

The personality of a nervous person is a self-centered defensive mechanism, and he strains every nerve to protect himself. When this becomes a habit, it results in distorted character traits. When we live in this society, we have various objects of anxiety because the society is not especially made for our convenience. In companies neither fellow workers nor supervisors are necessarily your best friends. Even if a student likes sleeping late in the morning, no school will change the starting hour from 9 o'clock to 10 o'clock. Everyone has to discipline himself to get up early.

In addition, there are unexpected traffic accidents, earthquakes or other natural disasters, pollution and thousands of different illnesses. We have anxiety about surviving such calamities, and this anxiety is a basic condition for all human beings. Even if one is not conscious of his anxiety, he still has it. If we do not have anxiety, we cannot protect ourselves from danger.

The objects of anxiety are countless, but each person places the most importance on something different. Some people are concerned only about their health, and some worry about the fears they have when they meet others. When you hear of unfortunate incidents, then you may fear that such things may happen to you. In this way, even one person considers different threats important, depending on the time and the place.

A spoiled person feels free at home, but once he is outside he feels great pressure from his surroundings. He is like a pampered greenhouse plant in that he feels strong opposition when he encounters the air outside. That is why a person who has been spoiled at home tends to have neurotic symptoms: his anxiety intensifies when he goes outside. Outside circumstances may be inconvenient for him very often, and it is nearly impossible to fight back against each one of them.

When you think of your own ability, it is never sufficient, and you have many weaknesses. Health is the same: not many people are tough enough to resist all diseases. Also, there are many inconveniences in one's social environment, whether in the family or at work. There are many such things wherever we are, and so it is very difficult to deal with all of them well.

A neurotic person in such a case tries to make as few enemies as possible, and he selects one shortcoming as the cause of his problems, believing that he would feel all right if he could eliminate it: "If only I did not feel this heaviness in my head," or, "If only I did not fear others." He wants to make it as simple as possible because of the principle of economy in the functioning of the human mind.

The objects of anxiety we humans have are innumerable, but a neurotic person selects that which is the most inconvenient to him and thinks everything is going to be all right as long as he gets rid of it. He sometimes chooses a ridiculous one, and even a simple obstacle can be seen as an especially threatening one for him. For example, when he reads a book, he sees his nose and feels it is in the way of his reading. He perceives the presence of his nose in his visual field as bad. Everything would be fine without this. It is simple: he thinks he should not look at his nose; however, because he thinks he should not look at his nose, his attention is directed to it. This mental interaction is contradictory: he tries to simplify his problem, but instead he gets trapped by it.

People who are anxious in the presence of others try to make their problem as simple as possible; they think it will be solved as long as they do not fear having a red face, or as long as they do not feel nervous in front of others, or as long as they do not have strange facial expressions. As these examples show, they try to focus on one detail.

The morbid fear of illness functions in the same way. We normally dislike all illnesses, but a neurotic limits the object of his fear to only one, such as cancer, venereal disease or Hansen's disease (leprosy). It probably seems to him much easier to deal with as long as he limits the object of his anxiety to only one. However, since he focuses on this one, his attention often goes to it, and the result is a reverse effect. This happens because, as I stated before, the distortion of the personality lies at the base of a person's neurosis. The distortion is to seek his own security in a self-centered way, and the negative defense mechanism with which he tries to protect himself from the outer world becomes chronic. Such a basic personality distortion causes his desire to simplify his defense by focusing on only one object.

The Meaning of Clinical Morita Therapy

How can we cure such problems? Understanding the theory can be a clue for restoration, but a neurosis cannot be cured easily by mere understanding. That is, the distortion of one's character cannot be straightened by simply comprehending the nature of the problem. Thus, one must change his attitude toward life as a whole.

Our personalities cannot be changed substantially merely by understanding with our minds. To change significantly we need to change our attitudes toward life in general, to acquire an attitude of being in touch with the reality of the outside world instead of being in touch with only ourselves. In the case of outpatients who are treated by Morita Therapy, there is no other way but to explain such points; but more serious cases of neurosis cannot be cured easily by using only such psychological procedures.

That is why Dr. Morita began to cure neurotics by full-scale inpatient treatment. In this case the patients not only understand mentally, but also hospitalization itself signifies a change of environment that can become a turning point. That is, if a patient stays in the same environment as before, then his conditioned reflexes cause him to do many things from force of habit, so it is better to change his environment in order to get him away from his old habits. If it is a special environment, an environment that is made to be convenient for treatment, then it is much better. The mere fact of changing one's environment by moving into a residential program has significance as part of the treatment. The simplest effect is a temporary reaction to the limits of hospitalization, but that reaction disappears as soon as the patient is released to go home. This example shows that some patients can be influenced by just changing their living conditions.

Not all neurotics can be cured by simply a change of environment, but it helps to a certain degree. Changing one's environment by entering the clinic, including a required period of isolated bed rest, is different from mere understanding. During their first week in the hospital patients are required to rest in bed without doing anything else. Bed rest means to rest their tired minds and bodies. Moreover, they feel bored while they are resting in bed since there is little stimulation and no outlet for action. Then the desire for action increases, and the wish to do something accumulates. That is why they respond sensitively toward the stimulation from the environment when they finally do get up. They may have fresh attitudes toward the outside world, which they have disliked up to that moment. Also, confinement in bed means having nothing to do but think. They have time to think of themselves and think directly without escaping from their pain. They cannot avoid their suffering, so they feel that they have to face themselves.

Keeping a journal after getting up also helps them to reflect upon themselves, and writing about matters of the outside world helps them to get into contact with reality. Of course, it also helps their doctors know the condition of the patients better, which results in better communication between doctors and patients.

In addition, there is a group living experience that is used as a form of treatment. Living in a group means that one cannot have his own way, so he becomes socialized. Neurotics, people who tend to be obsessed, lack socialization. This lack stands out especially among those who heretofore have been allowed to have their own way. When one has to live among many other people, he is not allowed to be selfish and just go his own way. Therefore, he naturally tries to refrain from asocial or antisocial attitudes. This is what it means to be socialized.

Next is work therapy (sagyo ryouhou). This is also an important part of Morita Therapy. By working, a patient can cultivate the attitude of doing things related to the affairs of the outside world. He stops being concerned only about himself, and his attitude becomes more receptive. Also, work therapy means to him that, even with his handicaps, he can experience working or playing if he tries. Working and other activity suits the real nature of human beings because our bodies are made primarily to be active. Our brain cells are always active, thinking or feeling something;

we cannot stop thinking when we are awake. Action makes a human being become the authentic self he can be.

As I stated just now, changing not only the mind, but also changing the character constructively as a whole is useful for treatment. Some people call Morita Therapy *gajoku ryouhou* (isolated bed rest therapy), but it is not only that. Neither can we call it Sagyo Ryouhou (work therapy) just because it involves work. You may call it *arugamama ryouhou* if you interpret *arugamama* in many different ways, but just reciting "*arugamama, arugamama,*" in one's mind does not work as treatment. To practice an *arugamama* attitude is important. Morita Therapy is a total approach which combines treatments that change one's physical and mental condition constructively.

Changing your character does not mean understanding only with your mind, but also confronting the outer world directly in practice. By doing so you can acquire attitudes toward life that help you to adequately manage your affairs in the real world. This is most important, and as long as you practice it your symptoms will naturally fade to almost nothing, even if you just leave them alone. If you wrestle with your symptoms, the harder you try to get rid of them, the more they will stick to you. Accept your symptoms as they are, and, as I said before, if you try to get in contact with the outside world, and recover the wholeness of your personality from the distortions of a self-centered defense mechanism, then you will improve naturally without even knowing it.

6

Seven Conditions for a Mentally Healthy Life

There is a man who suffers mental anguish over riding trains and buses because he thinks his stomach does not feel right. He says that his stomach fills with gas when he stands, and that he starts having pain around his heart and feels terrible. Hearing him, it would seem that there is something wrong with his stomach and intestines but, in fact, this person does not have any organic disorders. Then why does this symptom come about?

The first thing that comes to mind is that, as the term psychoneurosis indicates, mental problems appear in the body. Once there was an outpatient whose neck was crooked although he could move his body. Like pictures of people in ancient Egypt, his body faced the front while his face looked sideways. Orthopedic specialists could not find anything wrong with him. This was a special case, but it could be called a kind of psychosomatic disorder.

Our stomachs and hearts are controlled by autonomic nerves. Since the emotions and the autonomic nerves are centered in the same location, autonomic ataxia occurs when a mental imbalance leads to an autonomic nerve

41

imbalance. Different persons have different symptoms, but those which appear in one's heart are called heart neurosis; stomach disorders, such as gas noises, constipation or diarrhea are called stomach neurosis. The symptoms are different but they all stem from the same cause, which is a psychosomatic disorder. When you have such a disorder, it is important to live a healthy life even with the symptoms present.

Continue to Do Something Useful

The first condition of a sound mind is to be able to keep doing constructive work, to continue to do something useful. This is different from doing it sporadically. A lazy person is not mentally sound. Being able to keep doing constructive work requires quite a lot of patience, as well as an active spirit.

It is important to do constructive work because we do not live alone. We live in community, in relationships with others around us. In concrete terms, the clothes that we wear, the food that we eat or the houses we live in are not things that we made by ourselves. All of them were made by other people. We depend on others for our living. That is why we should contribute to others in some way, and those contributions make us full-fledged human beings. A person who cannot contribute to something other than himself cannot be called a mentally sound person. Of course, if someone cannot do it because he is physically ill, then that is a different matter.

See and Judge Things as They Are

The second condition for a sound mind is to be able to see and evaluate things as they are (*arugamama*). If one sees things wistfully or pessimistically in an unbalanced way, then it is hard for him to act appropriately whenever necessary.

When one is obsessed with something, his perception becomes distorted by the thing that obsesses him. For example, a person who is anxious about contact with others is obsessed with his symptoms, so he is very concerned about the opinions of others. He wonders whether someone may speak ill of him or dislike him. When he sees others talking, he thinks that maybe they are talking about him. When others are laughing, he worries that they might be laughing at him. In these ways he relates events to himself and passes judgment, even though he has no way of knowing the facts. On the other hand, to leave what you do not know as something unknown is what it means to see things in the *arugamama* way.

The person who is obsessed with anxiety about illness always questions whether he has cancer, or whether he is going to get cancer. If one is in this condition, we cannot say that he is healthy. After various checkups, if one is diagnosed as having neither cancer nor any special likelihood of getting cancer, then that is a fact; so he should clearly recognize and live according to that fact. That acceptance is healthy, but if one does not recognize such facts, and worries about whether he has cancer, then that means he cannot see things as they are.

Some people are too optimistic and see things only wistfully, but if it exceeds certain limits, we cannot say that they are really healthy. At first sight they may look cheerful, but they have difficulty adapting themselves to reality. One mental disorder, mania, makes people extremely optimistic. They feel that their ability is very great, they interpret things according to their wishes, and they end up failing. Such persons may feel good, but objectively they are not healthy. To be able to see things as they are is the sign of mental health.

Share the Joys and Sorrows of Others

Being able to love others: to rejoice in their happiness and feel sorrow for their misfortunes is the third condition for being a healthy person. Heartless people, cruel criminals, and people who practice antisocial acts that harm others are not healthy. It is common for humans to think that what is hard for one is hard for others, and what is pleasurable for one is pleasurable for others. That is why we do not like to see others suffer, and we are happy to see others happy. This is the social nature we have. People who are poorly socialized think everything is all right as long as they themselves are all right; they are only concerned about themselves. They become antisocial and asocial. As I mentioned before, there is social solidarity, and we exist in relations with others. One of the characteristics of a healthy human being is to have the social motivation not to harm others, not to trouble others, but to feel joy and sorrow with other people.

Have Self-Control and Self-Reflection

Fourth, it is absolutely necessary for healthy people to have self-control and to examine themselves. Some say that people with strong beliefs are healthy, but people with strong incorrect beliefs are troublesome. Of course, it is better to believe something with a degree of certainty, but bigotry is no good. There are people with strong beliefs who try to control everything with one thought, one obsession. The person who suffers from delusions of persecution is a typical example. He cannot reflect upon himself and discover that it is a delusion. It is necessary to be able to reflect on what one is doing and determine whether it is antisocial or not, or reflect on what he is thinking and know whether it is healthy or unhealthy. For ages it has been said that one who cannot reflect upon himself is not a wise man. This maxim is certainly true.

Take Responsibility for Your Actions

The fifth condition for a sound mind is to be able to take responsibility for one's actions. A small child cannot take responsibility for his actions. That is why if a little child behaves in an antisocial way, he does not have criminal responsibility and is not subject to legal punishment. Similarly, people with serious mental handicaps or those of unsound mind are not held responsible for antisocial behavior because they are considered very ill.

In the past, when a drunk committed crimes he did not remember later, it was believed that he did not have to take responsibility because he did not have a sound mind at the time; but today this is not so. Such a person may be the kind who becomes violent every time he drinks. He repeats such actions and still keeps drinking, and so he is considered responsible. Conversely, when a person does not take responsibility, it is just like admitting that he does not have a sound mind or is still an immature child.

A full-fledged adult can take responsibility for his actions. Therefore, if a person does not take responsibility for his actions then he is not a real adult.

Be Flexible

The sixth condition is to have mental elasticity and flexibility. In the Analects of Confucius there is a saying, "A wise man is not a pot." That is, a pot is convenient, but it has only one use. A teacup is good for drinking tea, but it is not very useful for anything else. A clock is useful to know the time, but it has no other use. A car is the same, and it is very convenient, but humans have to drive it. If the decisions are left to the car, then there is no flexibility. On the other hand, however trivial it seems, living things do not bump into electrical poles when they walk. In other words, they are flexible.

Among humans there are some who are obsessed or controlled by one idea, having no flexibility in their stubbornness. Once they decide something, they think they are absolutely right, and no contradiction can change them. Such inflexibility cannot be called mentally healthy. Paranoia is a condition in which one is obsessed with one idea and nothing else. This is in no way considered a healthy condition.

Understand Humor and Enjoy Life

The seventh condition, and this is something I especially want to add at the end, is the importance of understanding humor and enjoying life. Being serious is all right, but there are some who are serious and not interesting. A lack of humor does not necessarily make one unhealthy, but if possible it is better to understand and appreciate humor. One who cannot appreciate humor sometimes flares up when someone plays a joke on him. People cannot even tell jokes around such a person. People need some latitude to tell each other jokes and to make fun of each other. Humor in life is like a lubricant. It can make contact between people gentle and amiable rather than being cool and instrumental.

Only with the freedom to enjoy life can people be rich and happy. I think we can enjoy things infinitely if we have purity of heart. For instance, autumn has various natural scenes and objects that we can enjoy, such as chrysanthemum blossoms, colored leaves, and the singing of wild birds. We can enjoy reading books which satisfy our intellectual curiosity. Or we can listen to music, appreciate fine arts or enjoy sports. In any case, it is necessary to have the freedom to enjoy life.

In this way a healthy person has many kinds of traits, but among them some are more important than others. To be able to keep on doing constructive activities is the most important among them. Without this characteristic one cannot be called a complete, authentic person.

In addition, our personalities vary. For example, some people are good at speaking and some are not. Some people speak well and often, but being taciturn does not prevent one from being fully adult. There are many great people who are taciturn but, on the other hand, there are some who fail because they speak too much. There are some who are able to serve others by talking a lot, but there are others who make slips of the tongue and who hurt the feelings of others by talking too much. In this way, it is usually better to have various abilities, but it does not matter too much if you do not have them. Being good at drawing is better than being poor at it, but even if you are bad at it, that fact does not mean you are unhealthy.

I have enumerated many general characteristics of healthy people. If you think about these conditions in everyday life, then you will have an awareness of how you should live and what you should do to be a healthy person. If there is something contradictory inside yourself, then you should reflect upon yourself to find out what is wrong or overdone, and then you can become a healthy person if you control yourself.

It is a basic principle for a neurotic person to live a healthy life in order to become healthy. Living a healthy life means that we should apply our abilities and approach the outside world with correct attitudes. Neurotic symptoms cannot be cured by resting. In other words, if you lead a life filled with the desire to do, see, listen, and know, and if you are actually practicing what you desire and you feel you do not have enough time, then on the whole you are leading a healthy life. If you avoid struggling with and trying to eliminate or escape from your symptoms, and if you keep such a healthy life, then eventually your symptoms will disappear.

In Zen there are such expressions as *tongo* (sudden enlightenment) and *zengo* (enlightenment that comes unnoticed). Tongo means to gain enlightenment suddenly for a particular reason: suddenly your frame of mind opens up. This kind of thing occurs once in a while, but you cannot expect it to happen. *Zengo* means to gain enlightenment by gradually accumulating it, hence enlightenment occurs even though one is not aware of it. Neurosis is cured in this way.

While you steadily lead a healthy life, one day you look back and realize through your experience that you are nearly freed from old limitations caused by your symptoms.

7

Self-Awareness of Being Imperfect

"My Facial Expressions Disturb Others"

Many people who are anxious in their encounters with others are afraid that they give others negative impressions by their facial expressions. There is no way of knowing what others think, but this idea takes strong hold of them. They suffer from various anxieties, becoming obsessed with such fears. Their obsessions may focus on their body odors, the shapes of their faces or heads, and so on, but as long as they keep their obsessions, they cannot be cured.

Once there was a man who felt badly about the back of his head protruding. When I asked the reason, he told me his story. In his junior high school there was a teacher whose nickname was "charcoal-engine car" because the back of his head stuck out. The charcoal-engine cars used when there was no gasoline during the war had big humps in the back where they burned charcoal. Since the teacher's head had a bump in the back, his nickname was "charcoal-engine car."

The young man noticed that he also had a bump in the back of his head when he touched it. "This is terrible, I also have become a "charcoal-engine car."

It weighed heavily on his mind, and he started feeling that everyone was looking at his head. Strangely, he had never felt self-conscious before, but once he started worrying, he felt everyone looking at his head. You probably realize that his feelings were purely subjective.

Finally he went to a surgeon and asked him to scrape off part of his skull. He said the doctor had given in to his incessant demands and had done the operation. I could not tell whether the doctor had actually removed any tissue or not, but the man was relieved at the time.

However, this did not solve his problem. This time his sister said, "Your jaw is sticking out." He was worrying about his jaw when he came to me. He said, "Doctor, my jaw is weighing on mind, and I feel everyone is looking at me."

He had stopped worrying about the back of his head since he had undergone cosmetic surgery, but now he began to think about his jaw. He asked, "Doctor, should I scrape off part of my jaw?" If he did, he would have a blank face without features, like the surface of an egg, a comical sight.

As you can see in this example, any incident can lead a neurotic into worrying about something that he has never questioned before. He suddenly thinks that everyone is paying attention to him, looking down upon his strangeness. In his case, the neurotic symptom of worrying about the back of his head was only temporarily improved by surgery; he simply changed the object of his anxiety.

The cause of his apparent improvement by surgery, and of the reappearance of his symptoms, was that his basic mental attitude had not yet developed properly. He did not really get well. He had surgery, and he seemed better, but that was only superficial and temporary. His inner tendency was a distortion in his personality, the tendency to protect himself, and it had persisted in spite of the surgery.

This self-centered defense is a personality distortion. He was only interested in protecting himself, so he was very sensitive to stimulation from the outside world. "How do others see me and think of me? How do I look to other people?" Such matters really worried him.

Instead of attending to the reality of the outside world, he had an attitude of trying to protect himself from the stimulation, and so he became over-sensitive as a matter of course. His fundamental attitude had not been cured, so even if one symptom was eliminated, another one soon appeared.

Another man was cured from the fear of venereal disease, but soon developed cancer phobia. After many blood tests he understood that he did not have venereal disease, and his fear of it disappeared. Then he soon started worrying about getting cancer. This means he had some distortion in his personality in which his fundamental attitude was to protect himself intensely, even if his superficial symptoms disappeared by some chance. When such a tendency is not cured, if one superficial symptom disappears, there is a possibility that a patient will develop another symptom following some incident. That is why neurotic symptoms will also disappear if one's personality distortion disappears.

The Arrogance of Social Anxiety

Neurotics are somewhat dependent upon other people, and they worry about what others think of them. Yet the opinions of others are often hard to assess. Although they do not understand the opinions of others, still neurotics tend to believe that others think them strange or look down upon them. They try to defend themselves from the judgments of the world. In extreme terms, people with strong social anxieties think that no one should ever think badly of them. Seen from the other side, we can say that such a psychology is arrogant. The psychology of not wanting others to think badly of them means, in other words, that they want to be seen as perfect individuals. Properly speaking, they should be more humble. It may not be advantageous to have faults and weaknesses, and sometimes others may dislike us, but nothing can be done about that. It is better for people to believe that they are all right as long as they do the best they can do.

Another objection to this social anxiety is that one places more importance on his public image rather than his real self. He believes it is sufficient that others see him as good, regardless of his true character. Extended to extremes, it is no good to be seen as stupid by others although it is all right to be stupid. In any case, placing excessive importance on one's public image leads him to fear real contact with other people. That is why he cannot easily disclose himself as he is.

It is natural to care about the opinions of the world, and it would be strange to be totally unconcerned. If no one cared about the opinions of others, society would fall into chaos. However, this is strictly a matter of degree; some are neurotic and some are within normal boundaries. Anxiety about interpersonal relations is necessary to a certain degree. However, if one becomes too sensitive to accept the idea of others disliking him even a little, he suffers from disappointment, making himself depressed.

On such occasions he should disclose himself as he is and strive toward his immediate goals, even with his fear of people, his timidity or his nervousness. When one is giving a speech, for instance, the first consideration should be the content of what to say at the moment and how to say it clearly. It is important to leave feelings as they are at the time, whether they are good or bad.

I was afraid of other people when I was young. I think I probably spoke very awkwardly in front of people. I used to memorize everything I was going to say because I did not want to make any mistakes. Far from going smoothly, it usually went just the opposite. My feeling when speaking in front of a group was different from when I was at home thinking. If I got off the track by accident, then it was different from what I had memorized, so I would become confused.

In such cases it is not necessary to memorize the entire speech; all that is necessary is to commit only the outline of your talk to memory and to speak according to the outline. If you try to speak from rote memory and make one mistake you get all upset. A plan that is too detailed is much harder to follow, so you tend to get disgusted with it right away. Since neurotic people have strong desires for perfection, they make detailed plans in order to avoid mistakes, but then they cannot carry them out. If you simply outline your plans, then you should be able to put them into practice.

Neurotic Symptoms and Conditioned Reflexes

Among people who complain of insomnia and fear of interpersonal contact there are some who continually take medication. They say fear attacks them when they stop taking their medicine. This is a kind of conditioned reflex. To be released from such reflexes they have to practice self control while gradually decreasing the dosage.

I would like to discuss conditioned reflexes briefly. This is a theory which Pavlov developed, but we can often see conditioned reflexes in everyday life. In the evening my dog barks and jumps on me, but he does not act that way in the daytime. In the evening I usually take him for a walk, so he probably imagines taking a walk when he thinks of evening. This is a conditioned reflex toward time.

A dog salivates when it sees meat. If you set a large cover over the dog at that moment, the salivation stops immediately. The mental influence over salivation is such that there is no appetite when anxiety is strong; the dog is now more concerned with the cover, and the work of the gastrointestinal system, including salivation, stops. At Koseiin we use a chime to announce meal times, so when we hear the chime, our mouths water. To break this conditioned reflex we could repeatedly withhold meals after the chime. Then the reflex would not occur when the chime rang.

Neurotic symptoms tend to become like conditioned reflexes. A person with an anxiety neurosis has an attack in a streetcar. He feels afraid, wondering whether he will be able to see a doctor when he is so close to dying. After he has such an experience, the same feeling occurs every time he gets on a streetcar. This is a kind of conditioned reflex.

It takes time to cure conditioned reflexes. When I quit smoking, it had become like a conditioned reflex. I had a habit of smoking right after waking up in the morning, so I wanted to smoke when I woke up, even after I had stopped. It was the same way after meals. This desire continued over a period of several weeks.

To cure something like conditioned reflexes you must leave such responses as they are and live your life positively and constructively without being controlled by them, nor escaping from them. Then it does not matter even if you have such reflexes. The responses lose their potency, gradually diminishing to nothing.

Mistakes of Generalization

One of my university friends could not resist memorizing the prefaces of textbooks before examinations in anatomy and other subjects. It is necessary for students to memorize a great deal; however, the fact that he could not resist memorizing even prefaces showed his obsessive perfectionism. Sometimes it is necessary to look at the larger picture.

If one tries to perfect the details of something, he puts too much energy into it to do anything else, and the whole of his life becomes imperfect. For example, a person obsessed with cleanliness washes his hands constantly. He successfully cleans his hands by washing them, but he cannot do anything else. When he touches anything even slightly, he cannot but wash his hands again. His life becomes very incomplete overall. One always needs to change according to the situation, sometimes attending to details as necessary, sometimes performing in a rough-and-ready way. Sometimes when one is busy, he roughly completes something that he usually does with great care. Of course, it is not good to do everything in a rough-and-ready way because the quality of one's work may suffer.

We often hear of the error of overgeneralizing. If one tries to apply the same generalizations to everything, then contradictions will surely occur. When psychoanalysts try to attribute the cause of neurosis to repressed sexual desires, many contradictions arise; sexual desire is only one of an infinite variety of human desires. If one tries to apply one rule to everything, contradictions increase. That is why it is said that "The mind changes according to the circumstances, and the way it changes follows Buddha's teachings." If one does not try to adapt to the changes of the outside world, then it is difficult to live. If one tries to apply the same principle to everything, then contradictions will occur. To apply one's own principles to everything is a subjective, self-centered attitude. To adapt oneself to the conditions of the outside world is an objective, reality-centered attitude toward life.

8

Adapting the Mind and Body

When You Are at a Loss, Move Ahead

Many people suffer from anxiety in their relations with other people. They want to be able to speak naturally without becoming too nervous in front of groups of people. They also worry too much when they talk with someone personally. They get tired, and it becomes painful for them to talk with others at all.

Patients who suffer from abnormal fears of inter-personal relations are the largest in numbers among neurotics in Japan. Everyone has the same kind of fear, and these patients are only slightly different from normal people. Especially giving a first speech is painful for anyone. I did not like it at all when I was a student. I tried to escape from it as much as possible, and that is why I could not improve. This can happen to anyone, so it is nothing special. If you ask ten ordinary people, eight or nine of them would say they do not like talking in front of large groups. It is something we all must endure. Once you get used to it, you can do it without feeling too much pain.

There are a few who simply love to talk in front of a crowd, but such people do not necessarily speak well. Some who do not mind talking in front of people often give mediocre speeches because they feel that they can talk about something without first giving it deep thought. I am not a good speaker, so I did not, at first, even try to speak well, but I tried very hard to improve the substance of my speeches. It is important to think carefully and to emphasize speaking with good content rather than with good style. Even if one is very eloquent, a dull story can never be anything but dull.

It is human nature to become nervous in front of many people, and one cannot eliminate such nervousness from the beginning. The first objective is to talk as clearly as possible, even while one is nervous. I paid attention to that principle. I came to the point where I never even thought about being calm when speaking in front of many people. I do not even think about or hope to speak calmly because it is natural to be nervous to a certain degree. This is an *arugamama* attitude: accepting it without running away. When such an occasion does not match your ability at all, there is nothing you can do, but otherwise it is better for you to choose to do it.

Neurotic people tend to be very cautious and negative. They do not act unless they have confidence. However, people acquire confidence gradually through their experiences; it does not always exist at first. In the beginning they confront obstacles without confidence. When you wonder whether you should do something or not, it is better to do it. Of course, if it is wrong or too difficult, there are cases when you should not act. However, normally when you wonder if you can do something, you can. If it is impossible in the first place, you would not even wonder. Neurotics often escape from things they are capable of doing, saying they do not have confidence. It is not good to be so negative. That is why neurotics so rarely employ the abilities they have.

Kankei Nenryo: "Everything Pertains to Me."

When one suffers from a neurotic fear of eye contact (shisen kyofu), he strongly feels the gaze of people near him and he averts his gaze from others, disrupting his concentration on what he is doing at the time. There are also some who suspect that all environmental sounds or conversations among others pertain to themselves. Although they cannot hear clearly, they think everything is related to them.

In fact it is not so, but they imagine that everything has something to do with them. They are so concerned about protecting themselves that they find the outside world oppressive. That is why they become wary when others are talking, suspecting that these people are talking about them. They cannot have the attitude of *arugamama*; that is, they cannot leave what they do not know as unknown. When others are laughing nearby, they think these people are laughing at them. They tend to think that way especially when they are anxious. Such perceptions are overdone, and they can be considered somewhat morbid tendencies. It is psychologically healthier to think it is all in your imagination: that is, others are talking nearby, and you do not know what they are talking about because they are not talking loudly.

Therefore, the correct attitude is to leave the unknown as it is. It is wrong to try to settle it either way. Neurotics tend to relate everything to themselves, which is a self-centered attitude. That is why they are not in touch with reality when they talk with others. The reality is the topic of the dialogue or the business matter being discussed. They should get on with the matter, but their attention goes to themselves. They are always concerned about the opinions of others, such as what others think of them or how others see them. The psychology of interpersonal anxiety is nothing but being enslaved by the perceived opinions of others, and so they become very sensitive. They do not get on with the topic or business matters. Instead they focus on themselves and listen to others halfheartedly. That is why they probably fail to hear so often. They cannot come up with topics, either. Moreover, they become increasingly confused when they face others. The important thing is not self-awareness of their own feelings but an attitude of being in touch with the reality outside themselves.

Human Beings Are Adaptable

Fundamentally our minds and bodies are meant to be active. It is natural for a healthy person to be bored after a week in bed because our real desire is to exercise our abilities in dealing with the outside world.

There is a phrase, *munen muso* (freedom from all thought), but this is merely a symbolic phrase. When one is doing something intensely, his mind becomes one with the object itself. This is called *munen muso*, but actually it is not really *munen muso*. Rather, this is a state in which one's mind is acting fully. We use the phrase symbolically. In fact, our brains are made so that we cannot help but think or feel something when we are awake.

Our bodies are made to be active. In medicine the term atrophy refers to something becoming weak and withered when it is not used. That is, if one does not use his body, his organs gradually weaken and become atrophied. Muscles that are not used become atrophied. When one is in bed for a long time, muscles shrivel. It becomes hard to walk. They develop if used, so the leg muscles of athletes usually develop remarkably. When one kidney is taken away, the other starts working twice as much. In this way a function develops greatly if used, and it withers away if not used. In the same way our brains should be put to work.

Work makes one tired, and it becomes necessary to rest the parts that have worked. In everyday life there is little meaning in wasting time while one is awake. When one has done mental work, he should follow it with physical work, allowing his brain to rest. After work that requires heavy use of one's arms, light manual work will allow arm muscles to rest. In this way, by changing work, the human body does not require special times of rest besides those needed for sleep.

Human organs are made to be active all the time. Our hearts work without stopping, even while other organs are resting. Anyone knows that if our heart stops, that is the end of us. Living things are made that way. To make our minds and bodies active is the way it should be, so it is not good to leave them idle.

Humans belong to the most developed class of living things. We have the greatest ability to change according to the environment. That is why humans can live just about any place. We can live in very cold places near the North Pole, and we can live in very hot places, such as on the equator. Compared to us other animals are not as flexible; lions, for example, cannot live in cold places. Very flexible living things have the ability to live any place because they eat anything. Sparrows eat both cereal grains and insects; they are omnivorous, so they can live and breed in many climates. Some birds that live in tropical jungles come to eat only certain kinds of food. Due to the abundance of food they take to selectiveness among the extravagance. Then, if such food happens to disappear, they may perish because they have little adaptability.

Humans should change and adapt themselves to changes in nature. Otherwise, they cannot do good work. Sometimes we find people who do not understand that reality. For example, a patient was watering garden plants right after it had rained. When I said, "They are wet with rain, so you don't have to water them any more," he answered, "No, doctor. I made up my mind to water them once a day." He was trying to apply an inflexible principle to the outside world. (Actually, there should be subtle changes in watering potted plants. For example, unglazed pots dry out much more quickly than glazed pots.) Just as one decides how much water to give a plant according to the actual dryness of the soil, you cannot do truly good work unless you change adequately according to necessity. It is useless to try to control the outside world by your principles and your opinions. It is all right to have ideals, but trying to control the outside world by inflexible principles leads to stupidity.

Nature, Society, and Human Individuals

In the first place, the natural world is not made especially convenient for human beings; nature already existed and humans came afterwards. That is why life-threatening bacteria spread if left to nature. In the past, even during wartime, more people died of contagious disease than because of war. For example, during the Crimean War more deaths were caused by contagious diseases rather than by the conflict itself. When we plant flowers or vegetables in a garden and leave them alone to nature, they will probably be destroyed by weeds or insects. That is why we have to cope with nature, and unless we change appropriately we cannot adapt to it.

Human society is made by people themselves, but it is not made especially convenient for individuals. There are many competitors, and if left to natural processes you cannot adapt to it. We have to adapt ourselves according to the circumstances. In fact, we are actually making adjustments all the time.

For example, we Japanese have an immense variety of ways of bowing when we greet people; but, if one decides that bowing always should be done in a particular polite way, then it becomes odd. In principle one should be courteous and try not to hurt the feelings of other people. Such a principle should be valued, but the actual way of bowing should be flexible. It is improper to make a certain polite bow one's motto or to greet even small children with formal polite expressions. In practice it depends on the other person's circumstances. For example, when the other person is in a hurry, it is no good to repeat polite bows. On such occasions it is all right to greet someone simply. In cases of exchanging formal greetings, such as on New Year's Day, we greet others very politely. A person should modify his behavior according to the situation; otherwise he may have many awkward encounters.

Therefore, if one insists that something always should be a certain way, he cannot adapt. He should change himself according to the situation, as others do unconsciously.

Unreliable Evaluation and Intelligence Testing

Humans tend to think that standards are very convenient. In fact, life has become more convenient through the use of artificial standards. For example, in government offices the daily working hours are fixed. They could not increase their productivity if some workers began at seven in the morning and others began at eight at night. That is why it is necessary to make certain standards. Children below a certain age may use public transportation for half fare, and other such standards are established.

There are also standards for intelligence: someone with an IQ below 70 is considered mentally retarded. However, even if such a standard is imposed, one may question a score of 71 or 69. There is no strict boundary since it is only an approximate standard. Many years ago, in the psychiatry department at Tokyo University, someone studied what had happened after ten years to people who had been diagnosed as mentally retarded. The results were very interesting, and while reviewing them I felt that, after all, the value of a human being cannot be measured by mere intelligence tests. There were many cases of people whose IQ scores were under 70, so-called mentally retarded people, who were doing great work. Among them there was, for example, a man who had completed only elementary school, but who was employing men with higher diplomas.

Therefore, it is wrong to say that someone's intelligence is inferior or superior by the results of their school records or their intelligence tests. A school record is only a partial sign of human ability; it is not the whole. There are many people whose intelligence is supposedly superior, but who still cannot do good work in society. It is the same among doctors. I know, because I have been a doctor at a university for a long time. Some who were very bright at the university are not popular at all when they practice medicine. Many doctors who are prospering and building big hospitals are people whose university records were not very good. My students are the same. There is one who once failed the medical board examinations, but he went on to build a big hospital and is now doing very well.

The capacity for activity among people, their attractiveness and such do not appear in school records. There is a typical example in my home town. A man who was ahead of me in junior high school was given a model student award since his school records were very good. He graduated from Tokyo University Medical School, became a professor at a district medical school, and then started a private practice in his home town. He was a very bright man, but he did not have a large practice at all. He struggled for several years, but eventually he had to go to work for another hospital.

In my junior high school there was another student whose grades were so poor that he failed. He used to say, "I cannot do well at school because there is something wrong with my nose," and he went through cosmetic surgery. He said he was all right later, but he failed again. After all, his poor school record was not due to his nose. In many cases it is wrong when one attributes his failure or success to this or that cause. The same man later graduated from a medical school, studied several more years at a university, and meanwhile he received his certificate and started practicing medicine. He developed a large practice. He even became the president of a medical association. Given that there are such people, it can be said that academic ability and the ability to act practically in the world are different.

Failure in General Practice, Success as a Scholar

One cannot judge a person's value by looking at only one side of him. Just the opposite of the previous case, there was a teacher who did not have much success as a general practitioner; however he became a very great scholar. Professor Tahara, who specialized in pathology at Kyushu University, is the case I have in mind. This professor discovered the fascicle [bundle of nerve fibers] that transmits stimulation to the heart, and now his name is recorded in anatomy books in reference to Tahara's Fascicle. He was very good academically, but he was not popular as a general practitioner after his graduation from Tokyo University. Even we, his students, could guess from hearing him that he had not been popular as a general practitioner. When he was giving pathology lectures, he would say something like, "This disease sometimes can be cured and sometimes cannot be cured. Some people die from it." He spoke very bluntly, so of course he would not have been popular as a general practitioner. (*Translator's note*: In Japan, doctors rarely disclose bad news directly to their patients. It is considered wrong to tell someone that he has a fatal disease, for example. Most doctors would disclose such information to a member of the patient's family.) However, he later went into the academic world since he could not succeed as a general practitioner, and then he exercised his tremendous ability. Human beings have many kinds of abilities; some have opportunities to apply them, and some do not.

Hokinoichi Hanawa (1746–1782), the great Edo Era scholar of classical Japanese literature, was blind. In those days blind men ordinarily practiced music. Even today there are great blind koto players, but in the past there were many masters of the *koto* among the blind. However, Hokinoichi Hanawa was not good at music. He was tone deaf and simply had no talent at all. At last, he devoted himself to study, and then he displayed great ability. Since humans have a variety of abilities, even if one does not succeed in using one of them, he may do well using a different ability.

Beware of Perfectionism

Nevertheless, it is no good to keep changing jobs by criticizing one's present work. Once I had an outpatient who had changed jobs three times. She would quit a job before she even got used to it. She would quit within two months or so, complaining, "This job does not seem to suit my personality," or, "It is too difficult for me." Some quit working after a year, saying that it is too difficult or something, but there is no way that they can get used to a job in only one year. Some people quit when they feel that their superiors are cruel or that they are not kind enough to take time to teach them. If the job does not fit them at all, then it may be better to quit, but no one can adjust in a short time. When people do the same work for ten years or so, they become experts. There are many hurdles to overcome before one gets used to one's work. You have to realize more fully that society is not made especially for your convenience.

If you are too concerned about yourself only, you become very sensitive. However, if you deepen your interest in the outside world, then you will be freed from self-centered obsessions. It is important to place emphasis on dealing with the reality of the outside world, regardless of your feelings. Since feelings change like the weather, you should do what you have to do, whether your feelings are positive or negative, leaving them as they are.

When the desire for perfection is strong, one tends to say, "I cannot do it well enough." This is the worst possible attitude. Perfect conditions are rare, and so even if we can do only fifty or sixty percent of something, we do it. Everyone wants to do something perfectly, but if his expectations are too high for his abilities, his efforts will result in disappointment every time. It is good to expect just a little above your average ability, so aim just a little above normal. For example, if you are going to play mini-golf at Koseiin, and your normal score is 25, then you should aim for 22 or 23 today. If you aim for 18, you will be greatly disappointed.

Your adaptation to the outside world should be based on reality. Contradictions increase rapidly if you try to apply your own principles to the world. There is a difference between the way the world should be and the way it is. It is wonderful to have high ideals, but you should think of an ideal as something that comes much later. The reality is that you are far below such high expectations.

When one has neurotic symptoms, the gap between idealistic standards and actual ability widens by attention to ideals. As one becomes cured of neurosis, he reduces the gap between his ideal standard and his actual ability, learning a more practical view of human life.

9

Unpleasant but Necessary

Views of Equality and Views of Uniqueness

The most common form of neurosis is an abnormal fear of interpersonal encounters. However, people who have symptoms of this neurosis tend to think they are special, and when they think they are special they suffer even more. This principle is true in general, not only for neurotic symptoms. If you think that you are the only victim of a tragedy, then you feel very unhappy, but when you suffer misfortune together with others you do not feel as despondent. For example, you would feel very unhappy if your house were the only one lost in a fire, but during the war all the houses in the neighborhood were burned, and in that case everyone felt some solidarity. In such a case you would feel less miserable than if only your house had been destroyed.

The fear of other people is very common, and if you are ever hospitalized in Koseiin, you will know that, indeed, there are many people who have this fear. To be able to appreciate that your problems are shared by others is a spirit of equality (*byodo-kan*). If, instead, you think that you are the only one who is suffering, you have a spirit of

67

discrimination (*sabetsu-kan*). That is, when others appear to be talking calmly in front of people, it is discriminatory to think that you are the only one who feels nervous. People who discriminate in this way do not sympathize at all with those who can talk in front of people. Ordinarily we sympathize with others when they speak before people, thinking that they must be suffering because we ourselves suffer when we do it.

When, in the spirit of discrimination, we see another person studying, he seems to be studying easily. On the other hand, when we study it is very difficult, so we do not sympathize with others at all when we see them studying. We think they are fortunate to be able to study so easily. Ordinary people do not think that way. They know that they study by suffering and enduring hardships, so when they see others studying, they admire them, thinking, "They are studying hard although they must be suffering from it." That is the spirit of equality.

In the first place, human nature gives us much in common. There are individual differences, but we had better realize that human beings have quite a lot in common. The differences are comparatively fewer than the commonalities, so that which you do not like is usually something others do not like, either. Some like drinking very much and some hate it, but instead of emphasizing such individual differences, we should stress what we have in common. Otherwise we can feel neither compassion nor sympathy toward others. Sociability means to recognize and value the common elements of human nature, and by doing so we develop as social beings.

Anxiety Neurosis and the Autonomic Nervous System

Some people are very afraid of going out, complaining that they cannot breathe or that their hearts race; in fact, they almost never collapse, they merely feel that they may. This is nothing but a pattern of anxiety neurosis. Anxiety neurotics tend to be controlled easily by their feelings. When they have anxiety about collapsing, their sympathetic nerves become tense, and their pulse quickens. They naturally start thinking that they may have heart failure at any moment, and they fear dying. This, in turn, makes their anxiety stronger, so their hearts beat even faster. Sympathetic nerve tension or autonomic imbalances occur. They begin to experience various symptoms. Some break into a cold sweat, some experience trembling of their hands and feet, some feel powerless in their limbs. Some feel the rush of blood going up to the head, and some feel the blood rushing down from the head; there is a great deal of variety. The stomach and the intestines are controlled by the autonomic nervous system, so when one has fear, the functions of the stomach stop or one loses his appetite.

Many people have committed suicide at Kegon Falls in Nikko. I actually saw the dead bodies once. When I went sightseeing in Nikko, I looked into the bottom of the waterfall and saw two dead bodies on top of a rock, victims of a double suicide. They had been pushed out from the waterfall. They were far down from where I was, so they looked very small. Nikko is a famous place for suicide, and people who want to die gather around there. Mihara-yama in Oshima is the same. There are several other places which are famous for suicides in Japan. That is why in such places innkeepers can more or less tell, "This person came here to die." Usually when people arrive at an inn, they have large appetites and eat a lot, but people who go in order to commit suicide do not eat much. Once they decide to die, they have no appetite. Their digestive fluids do not appear and their stomachs stop working. They feel heavy in the stomach, and they probably do not feel like eating. I once heard from an innkeeper in Nikko that he watches out for such people, thinking, "This person may commit suicide."

People have individual differences, but they are all alike in their fear of symptoms. People who fear interpersonal encounters say, "Those with heart anxieties are nothing. They know they are not going to die no matter how hard their hearts beat. We who are afraid of meeting people have real problems because we have to contact others every day." However, people with heart neuroses would say, "Those who fear contact with people complain that they have a hard time when they see others, but their bodies have nothing wrong. They are not going to die from it, but if my heart stops, that is the end of me. How terrible!" Neurotics do not understand the seriousness of each other's problems, and they tend to think other persons have foolish symptoms, but they are very serious about their own symptoms. If they can merely recognize that their own symptoms are also objectively comical, then they have made great progress.

Symptoms Are Subjective

There are various neurotic manifestations: some people have various physical symptoms, and some have anxiety or pain, as in obsessive neurosis. However, every symptom is fundamentally something that can occur to any ordinary person who, wishing he did not have it, can then make it special, reject it, and become more conscious of it as a result. That process becomes a habit. Whenever he meets the same kind of occasion, such symptoms may occur like conditioned reflexes. However, the symptoms are purely subjective, and the reality is not really such a great cause for alarm.

The reality is within the ordinary physiological or psychological range, and there is no need to attach great importance to it. To take such matters too seriously is against the principle of reality being the only truth. Of course, facts have some truth in themselves, but everyone experiences such facts as stomach disorders, heavy-headed feeling, tension or a rapid pulse. Those are facts, but to take them too seriously is a failure to recognize the realistic range of experience as truth.

A boy who once came to Koseiin when he was 17 or 18 years old was very afraid of agricultural chemicals. I suppose it was a kind of mysophobia, a fear of uncleanliness. Personally, I think it is natural to be afraid of them. We do not fear agricultural chemicals enough, which is why pollution is spreading and causing harm. I should say we have to be afraid of agricultural chemicals. We should make the use of them stricter, control the amount of use, and prohibit those that are dangerous. These suggestions all come from the important thought that agricultural chemicals are fearful and dangerous. However, in his case it went too far. He strongly believed pollution existed where there was no danger. He could not eat fruit or vegetables without carefully washing them. He felt that they were covered with chemicals, and he washed them with soap. He would use up one bar of soap in only three days.

There is a necessary psychological process for humans. It is the feeling that agricultural chemicals are dangerous, or that heart failure is frightening, or that other people cause anxiety and so on, and to a certain degree it is necessary. Such feelings are not given needlessly since we can still say that fear is necessary for human beings. If we did not have fear, I do not know how many more people would die in traffic accidents every day. When a car is rushing toward you, you will be run over if you are perfectly calm and collected. Since you have fear, you try to avoid it instantly. If you have no fear of illness, you will not keep hygienic practices. If you have no fear of other people, then you may start speaking without reserve in front of anyone.

Some people have an illness called mania. They really do not have the slightest propriety, and they speak without reserve. They are very sharp and quick thinking, so their listeners cannot tolerate them. Such people may also speak the truth, which many people do not want to hear. When such people are in mental hospitals, they vigorously attack nurses verbally. They say extremely severe things and make the nurses angry. The nurses retaliate, and then you cannot tell which are the patients. Such patients have no fear of facing others.

As I mentioned above, something like worrying about illness, which is a neurotic symptom, is necessary for all of us human beings. It is necessary but unpleasant, like a necessary vice. And so everyone wants to accomplish everything without strain, study effortlessly, meet others without nervous tension, and be free of anxiety no matter what their physical condition. We think of these things, but inevitably we cannot deny the truth. The more we think of such matters, the more we worry. We worry double: we worry about worrying. We wonder, "Why do I worry so much?" Ordinary people care about these things. Nevertheless they do whatever needs to be done, so they become free from them without awareness.

Inconvenience: The Root of Invention

When we begin to do something, we sometimes feel very weary. When the weariness becomes worse, we do not want to do it at all. At that time we think, "I wish I did not have this feeling of inconvenience." We think we would be able to work at ease, and work more efficiently, if we did not feel bothered by the inconvenience of doing something. However, we can understand that this psychology of weariness is necessary after all. If we did not feel that something were troublesome, we would not invent all the devices that increase our productivity. Only since we have felt bothered by inconvenience has automation developed rapidly. Pushbutton automation has eliminated the need to handle many objects one by one, and such devices were born from the feeling of inconvenience. It is very troublesome to carry bricks one at a time, so wheels were invented from thinking, "Is there a way to carry many of them at once somehow?"

The ancient Inca empire is considered a Stone Age culture. I understand that they made castle walls using very large stones, but that they did not have wheels at that time. So I think they must have had a very hard time. I wonder if they had the feeling that it was very troublesome.

I suppose wheels were invented from the hint that one can move heavy things by rolling them on poles. Once wheels were invented people could carry several dozen bricks at one time. Then perhaps they felt it was less troublesome. It was still troublesome to move the wheels by themselves, so they had cows and horses pull them. Then they had to take care of the cows and horses, so they in turn became troublesome. So next they began to use steam, electricity or gasoline. Many inventions have appeared from the feeling that something was troublesome.

I have heard that Thomas Edison was once a railroad flagman. Although Edison wanted to study and read, he had to watch for trains all the time. It was very troublesome to watch all the time, so he wanted to automate the signals. That is how railroad signals were invented. If there is no possibility of invention, then one just has to do troublesome things with the knowledge that they are annoying.

If you try to do troublesome things without acknowledging that they are inconvenient, then you get into mental conflict by thinking, "Why do I find this so annoying?" You may develop an inferiority complex, thinking you are inept. If there is no possible convenient way of doing something, then there is not much you can do about it, so you endure the work while acknowledging that it is inconvenient. If you try to do it at ease without thinking of it as troublesome, then you get into a mental contradiction.

Most toilets today can be flushed, so they do not smell so bad, but all toilets in the past were foul-smelling. You could not clean a toilet without having the thought of how terrible it smelled. But one would get used to the smell while doing it, and the feeling would disappear. Likewise, if you try to do something repulsive without thinking of it as repulsive, then you get into a contradiction. Repulsive things are repulsive; you do them anyway. As time passes you often end up not feeling repelled that much anymore. If you try to do it without thinking it repugnant, when it is primarily repulsive, you develop an inferiority complex by thinking, "Why do I feel this way? Others can do it easily, but I have to do it very reluctantly."

Arugamama means to do undesirable things as undesirable. You may do it nervously or cautiously, but you get in touch with the present reality and go along with it.

Understanding, Practice, and Mastery

In most cases you cannot escape from the psychological processes that accompany certain things you do, so you do what needs to be done by leaving your feelings as they are and by understanding that such feelings are common. You do not try to change your feelings, but you proceed, along with your feelings, to the work that faces you. This is the attitude of *arugamama*, which is important to realize and practice.

It is important to see reasons in all matters, but it is more important to master something through practice. Even if you understand something in your mind, it does not mean you have mastered it. Of course, it is natural that if you understand something, it is easier to practice it. When you are told to do something you have not understood, it is very often hard to do. It may become easy to do when you understand it. At any rate practice is important; an armchair theory is of little use.

Neurotic persons do not act because they do not have confidence. Many of them are concerned about their lack of confidence, but no one has confidence in that which he has never done before. For example, even if I were told to cut someone's hair by becoming an apprentice to a barber, I would have no confidence. If I did it, it would be a great nuisance to the person whose hair was cut. You have to practice such things, and gradually you will be able to do them. Then you gain confidence. Barbers do the same thing every day without thinking about their confidence; however, they do not do their work confidently in the beginning.

In the case of swimming, when people first go into the water, they do not have confidence in being able to swim. You simply move your arms and legs, floating or sinking. Then you get used to being in the water, you lose your fear, and you discover that you can float if you move your hands and feet. That is how you learn to swim naturally. I learned how to swim when I was in primary school because there was a stream nearby, but I do not know how I learned to swim. While I was flailing my hands and feet, I became capable of swimming without knowing it. Then I started doing diving and such.

Neurotics avoid trying to do things because they do not have confidence, so they tend to become very negative. However, if they run away because they doubt themselves, they will never have any confidence. They do not make any progress unless they try things that they think are a little too difficult. People with anxiety neuroses should go out when they have occasion to do so. People who have an abnormal fear of facing others should meet people who are especially hard to deal with if they have business with them. By actually doing it they learn that they can do it. They naturally discover that something they considered difficult is not such a great thing after all.

It is important to understand through your own experience, not just by understanding in your mind. There is a big difference between what one understands in theory and what he understands from experience. No matter how it is explained, one cannot know what water is. He does not understand even if he is taught the elements of water and its molecular formula. But, once he puts his hands in water, he knows very clearly, "Ah, so this is water!" Such is actual experience.

While you are doing something, even something you consider difficult, it is not beyond your ability as long as you are doing it. It is important to have such experiences. If you do not like to talk in front of many people, it is normal. You get nervous doing it knowing you attract the public gaze. Unless you get nervous, unless you get a little tense, your brain does not react well. Also, your body does not work actively either.

When you are in an exciting situation you need the power of your muscles. Your brain has to work quickly. Your blood pressure goes up. Your pulse accelerates in order to meet the demand. Therefore, if you are concerned only about the fact that you are nervous, or if you think you should not get tense or blush in front of people, then these reactions are impediments. In fact, however, such reactions are natural. Accept them. You will feel a lot better. Instead of hindering you, they can make your brain work even more actively. Accept all of these as physiological or psychological reactions given to you from necessity and keep on moving ahead. You must not think they should not exist just because you do not like them.

Part 3

The Essence of Morita Therapy

10

Neurotic Personality Training

I would like to base this chapter on a neurotic person whom I know very well: myself. This patient was born in the year Meiji 32, or 1899. A difference of one year has made me a relic of the 19th century.

I was born in the countryside in Kagoshima Prefecture. My father was from pure Kagoshima stock, and my mother was from Tokyo. My family, a medical family, had only two children, my elder sister and I. As the only son I was spoiled.

There were many books in my house, and so I began to read a lot at an early age. Compared with other children in my class, I had a clear head full of knowledge. However, I was very immature in practical matters. The disparity was enormous. I could not do what other children, who seemed inferior to me, could do much better. On one hand I had an inferiority complex, and on the other I had a superiority complex in learning. I suffered from this contradiction since I was very young.

Inferiority Complex and the Beginning of Neurotic Symptoms

In middle school I had my likes and dislikes among the various subjects that we studied. It might have had some-

79

thing to do with my environment, but I had a willful personality so I worked hard at studying my favorite subjects but not at studying those that were distasteful to me. Especially in military training there was an army drill instructor who often picked on me because I was a perfect target. Whenever he ordered me to face right, I would turn my head left. He used to say, "Kora doesn't even know right from left. Even a cow knows right and left, so Kora is worse than a cow."

I was bad at army training exercises. I hated doing something without knowing the reason for doing it. I could not understand why we had to line up and go right or left, or why we had to make double lines. Also, I used to daydream during the class because I had a vivid imagination. That is why I did such stupid things in practical matters. I did not even know the order of presenting arms, and so I was often punished by being ordered to stand and practice.

The teacher was so uneducated, even in the eyes of middle school students, that he sometimes said strange things like, "After you go to go march..." or "Taking bathing takes away your fatigue." At first I was impressed with his polite way of speaking, thinking, "Indeed, to 'go to go march' makes you tired, and 'taking bathing' feels good." He also said things like, "When you go out scouting, you sometimes have to use your four-legged four legs," or, "There is one lone tree over there."

He said such things so often that I gave most of my attention to his way of speaking. That's why I couldn't tell right from left sometimes. He scolded me so often about the same things that I yawned, which infuriated him. Every time the military drill period neared, I started having heavy feelings and pain in my head. Such bodily symptoms arising from psychological problems are now known as psychosomatic disorders. Nevertheless, I still attended every class in spite of the pain, something a weak-willed person would not have done.

From that time on I began having neurotic symptoms and became afraid of facing people. Once when we had to choose someone to give a speech, it looked like I would be the one. I had to manage not to be chosen, so I tried to read awkwardly when the teacher called on me. I tried to prove that I could not give a speech in order to avoid being elected. I received second place in the election, so I did not have to give a speech. In that way I began to suffer real agony in speaking in front of groups of people.

Interestingly, however, my school conduct improved after I started having neurotic symptoms. The school records had three ranks of conduct: High, Middle, and Low. Until then I used to receive 'Middle' every time, which meant that my conduct was pretty bad. In the fourth and fifth grades I received 'High' in conduct, not because I had become a serious pupil, but because I had become quiet due to my symptoms.

Spiritual Enlightenment in Suffering

After graduating from middle school I entered Dai-Shichi High School in Kagoshima City. In the beginning I lived in a dormitory. Pupils came from all over Japan, perhaps because the entrance examination was held in Tokyo.

Having come alone from a country school, I had difficulty adjusting. A variety of symptoms began to appear. I always felt heavy-headed. Everyone wore a school cap then, but I carried my cap in my hand because I felt a weight on my head when I put it on. I had severe headaches sometimes, and I suffered from insomnia. I felt fatigued. I could not concentrate. I was afraid of facing other people. I suffered from many such symptoms.

I wrote down all my symptoms and took the list to the school doctor. He told me to tell the school that I should rest and not study because I had *shinkei suijaku* (nervous prostration). I remember him giving me a tranquilizer. The theory of *shinkei suijaku* in those days was that a variety of symptoms were caused by nervous breakdown as a result of overwork. Since *shinkei suijaku* was caused by overwork, naturally I should rest and not study. Because of his diagnosis I did not study at all for one semester. In fact, it was hard for me to study anyway.

However, instead of being at ease not doing any homework, I became more frustrated when I saw other students studying. I still had to take the examinations at the end of the term. Since it was not my real intention to idle away my time without studying, my insomnia and other symptoms became worse.

When I entered high school my school grades were very good, but by the end of the first semester my grades were far down, as I had feared. In my desperation I thought, "This is terrible. I don't want to stay back one year. I had better do whatever I can. I have nothing to lose. I don't care even if I go crazy because my *shinkei suijaku* gets worse." That was the worst time for me, but I studied, although I knew that my studying was not efficient. However, when the results of the examinations was announced, my record was much better.

That is how I attained enlightenment. The school doctor had been wrong to advise me not to study. First, I discovered that it was not true that *shinkei suijaku* would be cured by not studying. Moreover, I realized that I could study in spite of such symptoms, and that whatever I did resulted in something, even when I thought I was doing it inefficiently.

However, I was in a trying situation. Even now I remember taking my list of symptoms to the doctor. Many patients come to me with such lists. After I began to specialize in psychiatry, I found a passage in a German textbook which said, "Every patient who comes to a doctor with a piece of paper is a neurotic patient." I was one of them.

Although I attained some enlightenment that way, it did not mean my symptoms improved. I was still afraid of facing other people, but the other students did not know that I had such fears. I did not say much because I did not want to talk to people. I looked aloof from the world, and the other boys in the dormitory gave me the nickname "astronomer," indicating that my head was in the clouds. I was not aloof with enlightenment, but I looked smug because I did not want to meet or talk to anyone. In many cases other people are not aware of our fears.

Awareness of Mistaken Desires for Perfection

When I experienced such symptoms I attained a certain degree of awareness of their nature, but I was not cured. Not knowing what else to do, I read different kinds of books and concluded, "This must be caused by my weak will. My first problem is to strengthen my will."

I wanted to become a Christian, so I read many books about Christianity and listened to sermons by Rev. Danjou Ebina and Rev. Masahisa Uemura. It is not easy to enter into faith merely to cure neurosis. I could not find faith, so I started reading books about materialism. Materialism had good reasoning, and it was convincing, but it was far from solving my immediate problems. There was a time when I was deeply inspired by reading Bergson's *Creative Evolution*. Sympathizing with Nietzsche's *Superman*, I thought, "All the people in the world are fools."

Although I explored ideologies, I was still passive in practical matters. I didn't act fully because of my various symptoms. That is why, as I mentioned before, I tried very hard to strengthen my will. The method I took was to sneak out of the dormitory around two o'clock in the morning. At that time Dai-Shichi High School was located at the bottom of a hill called Shiroyama, where statesman Takamori Saigo had committed ritual suicide. On this hill behind the school was a forest. Big camphor trees grew thick, and the dense forest was dark even in daylight. I would walk there alone, determined to become a person who could keep his self-control no matter what happened. I was far from fearless. I was startled every time an owl hooted. I took that walk several times, but I could not get rid of my fear no matter how hard I tried. And I tried very hard, even though I was still afraid. It was not easy to walk alone in the middle of a forest at two o'clock in the morning.

I did other things to train my will. For example, I tried to climb mountains, intentionally leaving my canteen and lunch behind in order to test my tolerance of pain. I also tried bathing in cold water throughout the year.

None of these things helped at all to cure my symptoms. In the beginning I had thought they were caused by my weak will, but as a result of my trials I proved to myself that I was not necessarily a weak person, that I could do these things if I tried. Nevertheless, I could not be freed from all of my symptoms.

During my first year at Kyushu University I was afflicted by a skin disease. The skin all over my body became very dry, and it started to flake off in a white powder. There was no specific medicine for it, and I suffered for one year although I tried all kinds of remedies, including going to hot springs and such.

While I was suffering from the skin disease, my neurotic symptoms did not appear. In fact, when real illness is present, neurotic symptoms fade away. After one year I started to get better, so gradually I returned to the university. Though the neurotic symptoms were getting better, I had not completely recovered.

This weighed heavily on my mind. When I examined myself, it seemed that my greatest fault was that my desire to be perfect was very strong, that I was obsessed by thoughts of how I should be. I believed, for example, "I should go into deep sleep right after getting into bed," and, "When I study I should not have distracting thoughts, but everything should flow smoothly into my mind," and, "My head should be clear and refreshed all the time," and, "I should always feel good." Such desires to be perfect were strong; I was always obsessed with the way I should be. However, reality does not work that way. Even within one day one's moods vary. When we study we sometimes recall what we did the day before or imagine what we should do next, and often we cannot devote ourselves totally to reading.

When one is facing another person, he stiffens and becomes nervous because he wants to make a good impression. He has some fear of the person because he does not want to be rejected. Nowadays young people have dates more freely, but in those days young men became very nervous and stiff when they met young women. I was that way, and I felt I would not be able to love anyone all my life.

I had desires like, "I should be poised in the presence of whomever I meet," or "When I give a speech in front of many people, I should do it calmly without getting nervous." I tried to control everything by my own willful desire for "the way things should be," which was so strong that the contradictions in my life grew. I came to realize that the strength of my obsession prevented me from seeing and accepting reality. I could not see in an *arugamama* way.

Until then I had eagerly longed to attain harmony and peace of mind. I was always yearning for harmony and peace in works of art and literature. I came to the conclusion that such longing was keeping me from seeing my obsessed inner self. I gradually came to the understanding that all kinds of pain, anxiety, fear, irritation or disappointment are necessary, and that it is impossible to be free from them as long as we live. When I read the journal that I kept in those days, it clearly states such understanding. I could not learn from Dr. Morita then, but I can see that I was moving closer to Morita Therapy's *arugamama* without being aware of it.

Responsibility as a Doctor of Psychiatry

In our final years of medical school we gradually began to practice clinical psychiatry: we actually saw patients. I began to feel responsibility as a doctor for the first time. Until then I had spent my time reading books or trying foolhardy training exercises solely to solve my own problems. When I started clinical practice, I realized that as a professional doctor I would have to know illnesses, so I had to study medical science more seriously. From that time on I began to study very hard. Eventually my school records improved, and I graduated at the top of my class. At any rate, I was moving in a practical direction.

Having experienced various kinds of neurotic suffering, after graduating from university I chose to pursue a career in psychiatry. This career would give me more opportunities to contact patients whose afflictions were similar to mine.

After I finished my one-year study of psychiatry, I had a chance to give a speech about it at a general meeting of the Psychiatric Association. I was still afraid of facing people. My speech was only for ten minutes, but the fear of speaking in front of many professionals was so strong that the content of my speech did not matter to me. I could not listen to the speeches of the five or six speakers before me, and I gave my speech with terrible stage fright. However, when I asked an older colleague, he said, "If you can do that much the first time, that's great." Nevertheless, I wondered if it had been good enough. This incident shows that I still had some symptoms of my fear of other people even after my graduation. I began to give lectures to nurses and students, and it seemed I had chosen the profession to which I was least suited.

Two years later Professor Mitsuzo Shimoda (1885–1978), who practiced Morita Therapy at Kyushu University, came to fill a new position on the faculty. He rated Morita Therapy very highly. In his book, *Saishin Seishinbyo Gaku [New Psychiatry]*, written with Professor Naoki Sugita, he praised Morita Therapy, stating that, "It reached unfathomable heights in Oriental Medicine."

I was interested in psychoanalysis and read many books about it, but through my experience with patients I believed that it was too difficult to practice. Professor Shimoda introduced me to Morita Therapy.

I came to Tokyo in 1929 and began to study under Dr. Morita. In 1937 I succeeded him as Professor at Tokyo Jikei University School of Medicine as a professor. In 1939 I established the Kora Koseiin Hospital and started the work of curing neurosis. The foregoing is my case history.

Following the Desire to Improve and Develop

I had a strong desire for perfection; yet I was very timid. At that time I thought nobody was more worthless than I. I greatly envied heroes and strong people. I always worried why I wasn't born to be a hero or a strong man, but now I do not think that way. I came to appreciate the fact that I am timid. I cannot do good work if I am not meticulous.

However, a neurotic is too careful about protecting himself. He tends to be too defensive, so stimuli from the outside world becomes very oppressive. He is like the cowardly soldiers of Heike during Japan's feudal era who heard the sound of waterfowl and panicked because they mistook it for an enemy attack. If one is interested only in protecting himself, he becomes too sensitive. However, if one uses the fact of being scrupulous or being timid in dealing with the outside world, it can become a virtue. Unless one is scrupulous he cannot do good work.

I mentioned before that one's anxiety intensifies if he remains idle, without studying. Why do you feel insecure if you live in idleness? If you think carefully, it is obvious that one has a desire to improve and develop, so it is against his true will to be idle. That is why he becomes insecure. A person who does not become insecure or stays carefree about being lazy is worthless from the start.

It is good to consider carefully whether you have a true desire to improve and develop yourself. If you realize that you do have such a desire, and if that is your true will, then you must bear your suffering. You have to keep trying in spite of the insecurity. There is no other way. If you find that you really do not have any desire for improvement and development, then there is nothing you can do. Confucius once said that one cannot carve rotten wood. Likewise, if the human material is no good, nothing can be done if one is lazy. However, as long as we desire to improve and grow, eventually we settle down and do what needs to be done, bearing our insecurity and pain.

My mind was torn. I did all kinds of things, but I believe I kept trying thanks to my desire to improve and develop. In any case, I have been the kind of person who feels insecure about being lazy, so I have been able to grow in this manner. Now I think I have come this far without too many failures because of my neurotic character, and I am thankful for it.

I received Dr. Morita's teaching, and I, too, have treated many neurotics. I have written many articles, presented papers on the subject at conferences, and published English articles in foreign magazines as an attempt to reform psychiatry. Now Morita Therapy is widely recognized, proving that our efforts have been worthwhile. We want as many people as possible to be satisfied with their lives.

Flexibility to Adapt to Reality

As I mentioned before, we cannot remove insecurity or pain from our lives. It is inevitable. We cannot do anything about it. The reason is that nature and society are not made to suit our convenience. Nature existed first and people came out of it, so of course nature is not made for people. If we leave plants without care, weeds will take over or insects may harm them, no matter how hard we may try to make a flower garden. That is why we have to apply fertilizers, pull weeds, and exterminate harmful insects. Society was made by people, but not necessarily for the convenience of individuals. We cannot change our natural and social environment the way we want to, so we have to make efforts to adapt ourselves.

Therapy for neurosis means to learn to change and adapt according to the way nature is rather than thinking about how it should be. Of course, it is fine to have ideals, wanting life to be a certain way. However, neurosis cannot be cured if one has a faulty idealism or perfectionism or if one has an attitude that hinders adjustment to reality because of obsessive concern for the way things should be.

Confucius said that a wise person is not a thing. Certainly a wise person is not a mere thing. Things are very convenient. For example, spectacles are very convenient for us old people. Loudspeakers are convenient when we speak in front of many people, and glasses are good for drinking water. However, these devices are worthless for other purposes. Even a car crashes unless someone drives it.

However, living beings have the characteristic of changing themselves according to the circumstances of the outside world. Even lower animals change themselves. Dogs have lower intelligence, but they do not bump into electrical poles when they walk. That is the difference between living things and machines. We change according to changing circumstances, and neurotics can also free themselves from their obsessions.

Essentially, having a neurotic personality is not a bad thing. Neurotics have a desire to improve, and their wills are not weak. However, they expend much of their energy protecting themselves, and they are oversensitive. If they develop an attitude toward life that emphasizes managing outside matters instead of paying so much attention to their own feelings, then they become free from their obsessions.

Obsession and Breaking the Smoking Habit

Neurotic people are overly dependent upon their feelings. They confuse their emotions with the facts. Once I had a patient who was afraid of needles. She always felt that there were needles falling nearby, and she could not relax. Wherever she walked, she was afraid. The needles existed, not in fact, but only in her imagination. She was controlled by her emotions.

There was also a person who was afraid of cancer. He visited doctor after doctor. Even when they said he did not have cancer, he thought they might be wrong. He could not have peace of mind. His behavior was controlled by the feeling that he might have cancer. As in these examples, neurotics change their attitudes and behaviors according to their feelings. Obsessive behavior means that, on the one hand, people do unnecessary things controlled by these insecure feelings. On the other hand, obsessive inhibition means that people do not do necessary things because of their symptoms. Neurotics tend to regulate their attitudes and behaviors according to their emotions. That is why I always say, "Put your feelings aside, and do what you are supposed to do as a matter of course."

At first it is difficult. It is hard for people who dread uncleanliness to stop washing their hands more than necessary. They feel uneasy, with a sense of unfinished business. They cannot rest until they do it to their satisfaction. They say that they can neither be at ease nor start other work unless they finish performing these obsessive actions.

But obsessions occur as a result of feelings. Such feelings become habitual. They are like conditioned reflexes. There is nothing one can do about them. Here is another example: I started smoking when I was eighteen or nineteen years old. I liked it then, but ten years have passed since I quit smoking. When I quit smoking I had a difficult time for a while. In this situation I wanted to smoke excessively, according to the laws of conditioned reflexes.

If you have a habit of smoking, you impulsively want to smoke when you get up. Also, when you are stuck in your writing, you really want to smoke on such occasions. You cannot do anything about the desire to smoke. It happens inevitably and cannot be stopped. You can, however, endure the desire without smoking. Obsessions are the same. The fear of cancer or the fear of uncleanliness attacks your mind all the time. You cannot do anything about it. You can control your actions freely, but you cannot control your feelings.

As I said just now, you cannot do anything about the feelings of wanting to smoke or wanting to practice obsessive behavior. However, you can control your behavior. For example, if there is a delicious meal in front of me when I am hungry, I cannot do anything about wanting to eat it; it happens inevitably. However, I am free to eat or not to eat. Even if I want to eat, I can leave it without touching it by telling myself, "It belongs to someone else." On the other hand, I can choose to eat it because I can ask permission later. I cannot do anything about wanting to eat, but I am free to choose whether I will actually eat or not.

It was very hard for me to quit smoking, but I have never smoked during the ten years since I quit. I gradually forgot the taste of cigarettes and now I do not feel any urge, even when someone is smoking around me.

Obsessive behavior is the same way. At first it requires a great deal of endurance to avoid practicing obsessive actions. It's important to hold on and move ahead. If you keep repeating more positive behavior several times, then it becomes less painful to endure. After a month or two you may still feel the urge sometimes, but it goes away unnoticed. Obsessive ideas become ordinary distracting thoughts. Of course, anyone feels bad when he thinks about the possibility of getting cancer, but that kind of thought goes away unnoticed.

On the other hand, if you continue with obsessive actions, and if your attitudes change accordingly, obsessive ideas become more and more powerful. But if you continue to do things naturally, without being controlled by obsessive ideas, then your obsessions lose their power. They simply become distracting thoughts. The cure of neurosis follows this process.

Arugamama

It requires a great deal of effort to discipline a neurotic personality. Your efforts should follow your desire to grow. This is *arugamama*. *Arugamama* means, as defined above, to recognize the facts as they are and to follow your desire to improve and develop yourself.

Everyone has a desire to be lazy, to have an easy time. If you are going to start something only after your desire to be lazy disappears, then your chance to do it may never come. Although everyone has a desire to lead an easy life, *arugamama* does not mean following your desire to be lazy. *Arugamama* means to restore your true will.

Your true will is to strive to improve yourself, to do what you are supposed to do, even if you have a desire to be lazy. Do not resist your desire to be lazy, but leave it as it is. You have a will to improve. Act according to your true will. That is the real meaning of *arugamama*. In short, to discipline a neurotic personality means to understand the true meaning of *arugamama* and to learn from experience.

11

Release from Neurosis

How to Eliminate Self-Centeredness

I was born on January 18th, 1899. By some strange coincidence Dr. Morita was also born on January 18th. I feel that this was an act of Providence. Because Dr. Morita was born in 1874, there is a 25-year difference in age between us.

I have been treating neurosis for a long time. Although in my advanced years I have little energy for the direct treatment of neurotics, I feel that I can never get away from Morita Therapy as long as I live.

Neurotic Self-Defense

The self-centeredness of neurotics differs somewhat from the positive egoism with which some try to earn profit even at the expense of others. Neurotic self-centeredness is the negative kind with which they try to protect themselves. They sometimes trouble their families as a result of neurosis, but they rarely take antisocial actions. Because they are interested only in protecting themselves, and live as if they were confined in small places, they become asocial. Among those who fear interpersonal contact are some who are in their twenties though they live like old people.

They narrow their perceptions and concentrate on protecting themselves, so they tend to become very cowardly and sensitive. As a result of their singular interest in self-defense, they feel threatened by stimuli from the outside world. The outside world, whether natural or social, is not made to suit them. Few things are as they want them to be, leaving many unsatisfied desires. They become more and more sensitive to outside threats.

Moreover, neurotics who strongly desire to be perfect find various mental and physical defects in themselves. Of course, these defects are not so great objectively, but they believe them to be very serious. They constantly scrutinize their own mental and physical states. They look at themselves anxiously, thinking they may find something wrong. They are like measuring instruments for themselves. This shows the self-centered attitudes and lifestyles of neurotic people.

In this way, they begin to think that they cannot adapt to the outside world, and they begin to suffer from feelings of inferiority and helplessness. As I say often, everyone has an inferiority complex, but neurotics think they have especially serious and fatal defects, even if others think nothing of them. This neurotic way of thinking with its feelings of inferiority proves that they actually have superiority complexes. If they simply felt inferior, they would be satisfied by withdrawing into the present negative state. However, since they have superiority complexes at the same time, they suffer from dissatisfaction. They want to be able to act as full-fledged members of society, so they suffer deeply with their feelings of inferiority. They also have self-centered attitudes, so they think they are the only ones who have such special mental and physical defects. That is, they are obsessed with the idea that they are singled out and bound by their "unique" faults.

The Symptoms of Others Look Odd

I have found a great number of interesting symptoms among the patients who have come to see me. An example is the following dialogue with a patient:

[P:] Doctor, when do you wear a hat?

[D:] When it's hot I wear one to avoid the heat.

[P:] How about when it's cold?

[D:] Yes, I sometimes wear one to avoid the cold.

[P:] How about wearing a hat to avoid dust when I am cleaning my room?

[D:] I guess it's all right to wear one to avoid dust.

[P:] How about when I am cleaning in the next room?

This strikes me as comical, like a cartoon. Another patient asked me how dirty a handkerchief should be before washing it. The spectacle of a patient who fears uncleanliness so much and uses water so often that the water bill multiplies is like something from a comic book.

A patient once asked me, "Doctor, should I keep my upper and lower teeth together, or should I keep them apart?"

"Why do you ask me such a question?"

"Because I look absent-minded if I keep my teeth apart, but my jaws get tired if I keep them together." This is really silly, too. If you ask me what I am doing with my teeth, I really don't know.

Another patient asked me how often I swallow my saliva. I couldn't answer. I swallow when I am not aware of it. I am not conscious of it at all, so I can't answer the question exactly. He thinks about it all the time and asks himself, "Should I swallow now or wait a while?"

There are many more such cases. A twenty-one-year-old-woman who is now independently working as a full-fledged member of the community had a fear of emitting body odors. Patients who fear their own body odors are fairly common. They usually believe they have halitosis or other offensive body odors. In fact, I have never seen a patient who smells unusual, but the woman believed she was giving out gas all the time. I asked her, "Can't you tell whether you give out gas or not when you are taking a bath?"

She answered, "I don't think I give out gas when I am in the bathtub." She hated her flatulence so much that she covered her anus with a band-aid. You can say this is also a comical situation.

There was a twenty-year-old man who came to see me and complained about his eyebrows. He was wearing a headband to hide his eyebrows, even though it was a hot day in summer. The headband looked really strange to other people, but he did not care.

There was a patient who feared Hansen's disease, and he said, "Doctor, I am scared to walk under a tree right after a rain." I asked why, and he said, "Little birds perch on tree branches. The little birds perch any place, so their feet may carry Hansen's bacilli. So, the branches where little birds perch may have Hansen's bacilli. Thus the raindrops that fall from the branches may have Hansen's bacilli. That's why I am scared to walk under a tree right after a rain." His argument seems to be perfectly logical, but it is petty.

Relating Everything to Oneself

The symptoms I have mentioned seem especially peculiar, but the mechanism of these obsessions is the same as with other symptoms. They happen to be obsessed with something. It would be good if they could understand that the mechanism that causes their symptoms is the same as that which causes others' symptoms, but they don't understand it. When they hear stories of others, they think that they are comical and that these other people are stupid, but they don't find their own symptoms funny at all.

Once I wrote an essay with the title, "A Serious Comedy." In it I stated, "If you think others' symptoms are funny, that means you are looking at them not emotionally, but objectively and logically. When you see your own symptoms, they are not funny, and you really suffer." Of course, we doctors cannot deal with symptoms as humorous because we have to treat them, and we do feel sorry for the patients. However, if patients can understand that the mechanism of their symptoms is essentially the same as that underlying others' comical symptoms, if they can see their own behavior as equally comical, they will be quite free from the symptoms. To be able to see themselves humorously means that they can rise above their symptoms to a certain degree.

We humans have a lot in common, but there are individual differences within the commonality. We Japanese find novels written by Germans or Americans interesting. We also think *The Tale of Genji* and *The Tale of the Heike* are interesting. Doesn't it prove that the humanity of all ages and countries have much in common? That is why it is wrong to be self-centered and think that no one else has such symptoms as yours. If you recognize the fundamental mechanism as the same, even if the individual symptoms seem different, and if you free yourself from the self-centered feeling of being so unique, and establish a sense of equality with others, we can say that you have made great progress.

Neurotics are interested only in themselves: they habitually interpret everything, even accidental things, in relation to themselves. In Japanese there are terms such as *jiko kankei zuke* or *kankei nenryo*, which mean neurotics interpret everything as related to themselves. In addition, they interpret things negatively rather than positively. When someone is talking at a distance, they assume that he is talking about them. When someone clears his throat, they think it is intended for them, or when someone is laughing, they think he is laughing at them. People who fear their own body odor think a person next to them doesn't like them when they see that person rubbing his nose a little. Or, when they get a train, they think everyone is looking at them. This is an attitude that is obsessed by self-centeredness. That is why I often say, "You are conceited. Who is going to look at someone like you, who came from who knows where? To be stared at by someone you would have to work like a one-man band." However, they do not understand what I say.

Self-Oriented and Reality-Oriented Attitudes

Symptoms caused by self-centeredness have numerous characteristics. Since neurotics continually live in strained circumstances, various symptoms appear. They take questions of little importance as serious, and they are always concerned about themselves. I call such attitudes self-oriented.

How can people be released from such self-oriented attitudes? The answer lies in practicing and mastering an attitude of being in touch with the outside world. This is called a reality-oriented attitude, which means, in short, liberation from self-centeredness.

Since neurotics have egocentric attitudes, they think it is foolish to work. Work is very good for the treatment of neurosis, and it is one of the main elements of Morita Therapy. However, some work only because they want to cure their illness. Their attitude shows that their main concern is themselves. "I did this much work, but I have not been cured yet." It is as if they are checking a cutting they have planted by pulling it out every day and saying it does not have any roots yet. It may be inevitable to think the work they do is for their treatment, but it is important that, once they start to work, they should forget about the treatment and try to fulfill the purpose of the work itself.

Dr. Morita was ill in his last year, and he was in bed upstairs. Whenever he heard a patient sweeping a room, he would say, "That patient is getting much better," or, "That patient is not improving."

I asked, "How do you know that?"

He answered, "A person who is not improving works mechanically. He works with the attitude that as long as the work gets done, it's okay. But a person who is getting well changes his pace because he is paying attention to what he is doing. That is, when he is cleaning different parts of a sliding door, he varies his motion, and so the sound is different."

An attitude that is in touch with external realities and an attitude to work mechanically for treatment are different. One day a patient was cutting a hardwood log with an old, dull saw. His work was very inefficient. I asked him, "What are you going to make?"

He answered, "I am not making anything."

"Then why are you doing it?"

"I am doing it to cultivate my patience." If someone is working to train his power of patience, then in most cases he is working for himself. It proves that he is not in touch with what he is doing.

There was a wisteria trellis where flowers bloomed beautifully. One day a patient was sitting on a rock under the trellis. I asked what he was doing. He said, "There is no end to my work when I am sitting here. Every time a wisteria blossom drops, I pick it up and throw it away." I could see there was no end to his work, but it was not necessary for him to clean the wisteria blossoms one by one because the fallen blossoms are quite exquisite. In the tea ceremony they sometimes intentionally drop fallen leaves or flowers after cleaning the ground. He did not have to discard the wisteria flowers. His attitude came from mechanically thinking that he simply should work; it was not based on reality. He was not trying to fulfill the purpose of things.

Some people theorize about everything, but Dr. Morita used to talk about the importance of sensory experience. It means that if you use your senses as you work, you may produce better results. For example, when you look into a mirror, it just doesn't feel right to see a stubbly beard, so you shave.

At one time a lily was blooming in my garden. I thought the stem would break at any moment since it was so thin. So I asked a patient, "Please prop up that lily because it looks like it might fall down." I looked at it after he had finished. He had tied the lily to a short log that was ten centimeters in diameter. That was proof that he was confined by theory instead of using his senses.

Once Dr. Morita talked about being one with the thing itself. For example, when you see a ten-yen bill blowing away in the wind (in those days a ten-yen bill had great value), you try to catch it by jumping up instantly. That is the mental attitude of being one with the thing.

Tanbanokami Yagyu (a great swordsman) once sent a letter to the monk Takuan in which he talked about the attitude of being alert. He said it means that you answer "*Hai!*" [yes] immediately when your name is called. If you answer, "*Haaaa---i*," after you pause to wonder why you are being called, that is no good.

An attitude of being one with the thing means that you become one with the stimulus. When dealing with the outside environment, you make it your sole purpose, and then you do not keep asking unnecessary questions about purpose. As a result, work therapy supports treatment, but if you are going to work solely for treatment from the beginning, then, as just mentioned, the work can be very mechanical and inefficient.

To Take Action and Become Socialized

In the case of studying, some people decide to start studying only after their desire to do so fully matures. Those people are usually not good at studying. Study [*benkyo*] in Chinese characters is written as endeavor and force. It is not necessarily very interesting or fun. So if you want to start studying, you simply must act first. No matter how you feel, just sit at the desk, put a book in front of you, open it and read. By such actions your willingness to read may gradually mature.

On a cold winter morning it is very hard to get up. So if you are going to get up after your desire to do so fully matures, then you are going to be late. If you have to get up, just jump out of bed regardless of your feeling, and then your desire to stay in bed a little longer disappears. Thus, your feelings change according to your behavior. With work it is the same way: act first. If you start to work after your desire to work fully matures, then you become a lazy person.

Also, when you work, if you start doing whatever you find easy to do, then you gradually develop a rhythm of activity while you are doing it. If you try to work on a difficult problem from the beginning, and have a hard time, you may give up the whole job because you do not want to do it. If you leave a difficult part until later and start an easier part first, then you get into a rhythm. At the end you can often break through the difficult part.

I would like to discuss reality-oriented attitudes toward conversation. A person who fears interpersonal contact becomes obsessed by his own existence when worrying about what people think of him, how they see him, how he speaks, the expression of his eyes, whether his face is red, and so on. It is difficult for people to place importance upon two things at the same time, so a person who is self-centered and who cares about his own image cannot listen to others well. He cannot find conversational topics, and he is especially confused when he must face others. Reality-based conversation means to leave one's fear of people as it is, and to try to get on with the topic by asking questions according to one's desire to learn.

When one is self-centered, he tends to withdraw into himself. It becomes hard to keep any kind of social life. That is why many people are so asocial. In my own case I was far from being practical, perhaps because I was the only son of a doctor. I read many books, and I knew much more than my junior high school classmates, but I was very poor at dealing with practical matters. As I mentioned before, I had a hard time because of it. From my own experience I can say that people should have as much social life as possible.

One of the objectives of our inpatient treatment is socialization. Patients in our hospital live with more than ten others. They cannot avoid becoming socialized thanks to the many occasions to be together for work or play. That is one of the advantages of inpatient treatment. The self-centered attitude among neurotics comes from being poorly socialized in many ways. It is important to have as many opportunities as possible for socialization.

For example, if you are a student, I think it is good to join a club activity that you think you can do. It is important to do group sports and become active and useful in your club. If a person becomes useful in his environment, then people begin to value him. This is the same in a family, in a school, or in society. There is a saying, "A laggard hesitates to ask for a third serving." It means that a lazy person is someone who, because he is dependent and useless, feels insignificant and restrains himself from asking for a third serving. It is important for a human being to be useful wherever he is. If he becomes worthy, he will be freed naturally from his self-centered attitude. He will begin to feel comfortable with the fact that he is alive. Others recognize him, the boundaries of his activities expand, and he himself becomes greater.

To Enrich One's Life as a Whole

I once wrote a book called *The Problem of Love* [*Aijo no Mondai*]. If there is no love, a person's life becomes very empty. This is very important; a life without love is very dry and poor, even if one has great wealth and power.

How does love come about? Of course, with only the idea "I should love" one cannot love easily. One day a school teacher came and complained to me, "I know I should love all the students equally. I am suffering because I cannot do it no matter how I try. I don't think I am qualified to be a teacher." I think the idea of loving everyone equally is wrong. If fifty children are present, they have all kinds of personalities. Some are dirty, some are cute, some are naughty, and they are all different. Some are amiable, and some look mean. There is no way you can love them equally. So accept your feelings as they are. If you dislike someone, accept that as a fact. If you think of amiable people as likable, that is all right, too. However, as a teacher you have to educate all of them. Even if you do not like some, you still have to take care of them, so you do it. While you are taking care of them, you gradually begin to like them. This is a natural development.

We have a dog who was given to us by Dr. Abe, the Koseiin Hospital director. Dr. Abe did not know what to do with the dog, so he gave him to me. It is a mongrel without any special good points. His fur is long and looks dirty. I am ashamed to walk him, but he loves to walk. When he sees me in the evening, he barks for me to take him for a walk, so I feel that I must take him out. Although he is an ugly dog, I feel love toward him after many years of taking care of him. We wanted to have a handsome dog. Once we bought such a dog, but the two dogs did not get along with each other. We gave up the handsome dog, and we still keep this ugly dog. In this way caring brings out love naturally.

As with the school teacher I mentioned before, a feeling of liking or disliking someone is there from the beginning. You instantly like some people for no special reason, and dislike others the same way. However, even if you have to associate with these others reluctantly, you may eventually find them better than you had thought. There is a saying that a mother loves her foolish son most. When mothers take more time caring for their children, they usually start to feel love toward them, no matter how bad they are. That is the natural way.

It is important to take good care of things, too. Recently I have felt that handling things roughly can lead to the destruction of human love. Dr. Morita valued things highly. He used to talk about using things to their limits, giving them new life. You become more attached to the things you have used for a long time. In that sense I often see foreign people cherish the furniture that their ancestors used.

It is the same with plants. I like plants, and I take care of many different varieties. Of course, some people think that it is much easier to have a gardener plant fine plants, but I think you have a special attachment to the ones that you plant yourself. If you water and fertilize them yourself, your love toward the plants deepens.

By taking care of people or things or animals or plants, and by trying to nurture them well, you will surround yourself with people and things that you love. I believe that is the meaning of a rich life. An abundant life starts when one is free from self-centeredness, being thankful for day-to-day life.

To be freed from neurotic symptoms, you should become actively involved in what is happening around you; try to take care of things in the outside world, and deal with them well, regardless of your feelings. If you develop a life attitude that values these things, your symptoms will disappear naturally. When you try to fight your symptoms head-on, the harder you work at treating them, the more you get trapped by them, and you will end up with nothing. Instead, if you try to improve your whole life, your symptoms disappear naturally. I believe that this is the way to be free from the self-centeredness of neurosis.

12

The Causes of Neurotic Symptoms

Symptoms and the Course of Treatment

Dr. Shoma Morita's theory of neurosis is already widely known, and the overall picture is made clear in *The Complete Works of Shoma Morita* (*Morita Shoma Zenshu*, 7 Volumes, Tokyo, Hakuyosha, 1975). Rather than discuss Morita Theory itself, I will focus on my understanding of neurosis and the course of treatment derived from his theory, emphasizing the unique characteristics of Morita Therapy.

Adaptation Anxiety

Nature existed before people, and it is not necessarily made to be convenient for us. Every year natural disasters occur, life-threatening bacteria spread. If you plant seeds, the plants are attacked by harmful insects or weeds if left neglected. The society in which we live is made for us to live comfortably, but it has many defects. It is definitely not made for your own convenience. School does not begin late for students who cannot make it on time, and not all of your colleagues or your superiors have good feelings toward you. You can find limitless objects of anxiety in human relations, the economy, the insecurity of politics, pollution, illness, wars, traffic accidents, and so on.

We imperfect human beings who live in such anxious circumstances have many physical and mental weaknesses or defects. When we look upon ourselves, we often feel that we have various weaknesses in our health or personalities or abilities. I believe we all share a basic anxiety connected to human life: our concern about whether we can adapt to the natural environment, which was not necessarily made for our convenience, and to society, which is not especially in favor of us. We wonder if we can survive.

This adaptation anxiety differs in degree among individuals, and there are many differences in our objects of anxiety. Even within the same person the strength of anxiety differs, depending on internal and external circumstances. It seems that the degree of adaptation anxiety also has something to do with one's predispositions. Some people are cheerful and naturally optimistic, and some are gloomy and natural worriers. Even though we cannot ignore the fact that predispositions may influence anxiety, generally it has much more to do with acquired circumstances. Professor Mitsuzo Shimoda took this position in the early days of psychological research.

Recently the environment in which neurotics have been brought up has been regarded as important, but Dr. Morita did not show much interest in this. When he treated neurotics, he did not care about their childhood environment, which nobody could change. When patients were told that the way their parents educated them contributed to the occurrence of their neurotic symptoms, some of them placed the responsibility on their parents, turning the blaming of their parents into everyday work. Placing blame on something they cannot control does not help their progress at all. It is important to improve the family environment to prevent the further occurrence of neurosis, but we should keep our eyes out for patients who exaggerate its significance.

Self-Centered Defensiveness and the Objects of Anxiety

When adaptation anxiety is very strong, it is natural to have a self-centered defensive attitude because of brooding about one's physical and mental condition and vigilance toward the outside world. If that kind of defensive attitude becomes habitual and chronic, it is a character distortion or deformity. Specialists who see neurotic patients recognize that they try to defend themselves day in, day out. When one is planning a course of treatment, it is important to keep in mind that the cause of neurosis is based on this character distortion, which is a self-centered defensive attitude. Morita Theory focuses on trying to train the patient's character as a whole.

Human feelings themselves do not have any direction. Nevertheless, we often experience the fact that a feeling attaches itself to something when a patient is pushed about by anxiety or depression. Some depressed patients exaggerate the significance of simple constipation and become pessimistic, regarding it as fatal. Some regard insomnia as serious. In "pseudo-depression," if patients cannot find something to worry about at the moment, they get depressed about some small failing several years in the past, something they cannot reverse. When neurotics feel strong adaptation anxieties following an unpleasant incident, their insecure feelings concentrate on the incident as an anxiety object, and become set as superficial neurotic symptoms. For most ordinary people such incidents are insignificant, simply common experiences.

A student whom I treated suffered from the symptom of being unable to continue reading a sentence because his eyes kept trying to read the next sentence. Anxiety about one's nose protruding is the same kind of thing. When one pays attention to something, it is common that the thing attracts more attention. Symptoms become hardened when patients have defensive attitudes that are strong in adaptation anxiety. They are very sensitive to anything that prevents them from doing what they want to do. They are controlled by repulsion-negativism, which leads to what Dr. Morita called *kikko sayo* (psychological antagonism or psychic interaction).

If you pay attention to a thing in the outside world or a mind-body phenomenon of your own, you become conscious of its existence, but it disappears if you leave it as it is. That is a normal psychological process. However, if you consciously try to exclude it as something disadvantageous for you, then it gets fixed there and becomes a symptom. Why does it become a symptom? Because there is a problem in one's basic attitude. The superficial differences among objects of anxiety are not important, whether they are manifest as fear of interpersonal contact, fear of uncleanliness, feelings of heaviness in the head, insomnia or illness phobias.

A Theory of Defensive Simplification

I would like to address the fact that neurotics try to reduce the number of objects of anxiety. As just mentioned, there are numerous things that can be objects of anxiety, but a neurotic patient chooses to care about only one kind of illness on which to focus. Normal people are not overly concerned about illness, but even if we care, we do not limit our concern to only one illness. On the other hand, neurotics characteristically pay attention to only one kind of illness, such as syphilis, cancer, Hansen's disease or mental illness. When their attention moves to cancer from syphilis, then they don't care about syphilis at all.

People who fear interpersonal contact tend to specialize by worrying about blushing or the effects of their eye behavior upon others, or by feeling restless because of the gaze of other people. Even among patients who fear that they have body odor, many select only one kind of odor, such as anal, genital, underarm or breath odors.

How should we interpret this kind of phenomenon? We can say that in our actions and thoughts, whether we are conscious of it or not, we desire to achieve our goals without much labor, using the principle of least effort. It is very difficult to avoid or to defend ourselves from everything that can be objects of anxiety. We have too many enemies, and we are too powerless to deal with all of them. You can imagine how strong this helplessness could be among neurotics, who have self-centered, defensive attitudes.

So how do they solve this difficult problem quickly? According to the principle of least effort, they narrow their attention down to one target, consciously or unconsciously thinking that if this one problem is solved, then everything else will be all right. Thus, they focus on one thing related to their unpleasant experience in everyday life. They think that everything will be all right as long as they can get rid of it. This may look easy superficially, but it is a pitfall that leads to a mechanism which Dr. Morita called "a contradiction in thoughts," psychic interaction or antagonism.

Making the Means the End

If you look at psychological processes from different angles, you will notice many interesting facts. I would like to discuss a patient's symptom of being unable to read because of distracting thoughts. Such thoughts could be specific ideas, or they could be a symptom in which his attention drifts toward things on the desk other than the book he is trying to read. If he thinks this tendency is an obstacle and simplifies the problem by thinking that he must merely eliminate his extraneous thoughts for his study to go smoothly, then his efforts come to have a reverse effect. His efforts to rid himself of his random thoughts result in more awareness of his thoughts, and it becomes even harder for him to read. It is a vicious cycle.

When we read, we do not usually concentrate totally from beginning to end. Distracting thoughts inevitably appear, but we simply accept them and continue to read, although our minds sometimes drift away. We do not usually try to resist our thoughts, so we do not have to be too conscious of them. However, for one who has an obsessive fear of distracting thoughts, avoiding such thoughts becomes his main purpose. The avoidance leads him away from his immediate objective of reading a book. That is, originally the thing which should be merely a means to an end replaces the main purpose. This mistaking of the means for the end pulls him off the constructive right track and leads him into chaos.

Let us consider the dialogue of a patient who fears interpersonal contact. The immediate concern in a dialogue should be the topic or the business at hand. Such a patient, however, is obsessed by self-centered thoughts of what the other person is thinking about him, how he looks, his own blushing or his facial expressions, or his awkwardness. In short, he is obsessed with himself. As a result, his immediate objective is replaced by the idea that he should not have such fears.

As a basic principle of human psychology, one cannot focus attention on two things at the same time, so such people cannot hear others or contribute topics when they are confronting others. As a result, they become confused. Making the means the end exacerbates the difficulty of adaptation.

Moreover, the fact that a patient focuses only on his object of anxiety, thinking that ridding himself of it will solve all of his problems, will lead him to the thought that the object is great enough to threaten his very existence. However, the symptom that he regards so seriously is objectively a trivial matter, developed from the primary desire to live.

I consider this phenomenon a matter of making a partial weakness into a disaster because the patient regards it as a life-or-death matter. This kind of thing happens especially to youngsters. We often find a youngster who thinks he is worthless because he is not good at mathematics, or because he cannot get into the school he wants, so his whole life is irreparable. I should say this is a neurotic attitude.

I think an "estranging process" helps to explain the formation of neurotic symptoms, too. If an alien substance enters a human organ, an inflammation surrounds the substance. Even if it does not go into the organ, but merely adheres to it, we feel uncomfortable until we grow accustomed to it. We experience this when we wear false teeth or glasses for the first time. As we get used to them their strangeness disappears and they become one with us. When we interpret this strangeness more widely, I think it helps to explain the formation of various conflicts of human psychology.

Saliva is a necessary substance and basically a part of the body. It does not feel alien. Nevertheless, there is a symptom in which a patient is always conscious of the existence of saliva in his mouth and experiences it as an alien substance. Such a patient worries over the problem of how much saliva is collected, and then whether he should swallow or spit. He experiences his own saliva as an alien substance. The same kind of mechanism happens with mental phenomena as well.

We perceive our bodily functions as normal, not as something alien. Nevertheless, these functions are not necessarily pleasant; they are rather unpleasant fairly often. If, because of anxiety or disgust, we treat our normal psychological and physiological functions as alien or try to rid ourselves of them, we will become obsessed by them.

When I talk to patients, I use other explanatory terms like *rettokan tousha* (inferiority complex projection), or *taihi shigeki* (unnecessary comparison of stimuli), and I explain to them that these have certain functions to create neurotic symptoms. I think these explanations help patients to see into their own psychology.

Arugamama in the Course of Treatment

When we treat neurosis, we tell the patients that it is not an organic disease. We explain different examples of symptoms so that they can understand the nature of their neurosis better. We make it clear that, judging from their symptoms, there is no other way to be released than by acquiring *arugamama*. I have already explained *arugamama* before, so I will discuss it only briefly here, using for an example the fear of interpersonal contact.

If an anthropophobic patient avoids other people, it is giving up, not *arugamama*. Some give up trying to meet other people and stay home, and so there is no way they can be cured. They create artificial fears that confronting people is effeminate. Or they decide to gather up their courage and see others calmly by repressing their fears. As I have mentioned many times before, this approach produces the contrary effect of making them more acutely conscious of their fear of others. If one already has such tendencies, he reflexively feels afraid of facing people, and it is close to impossible to rid himself of this fear. If he is going to have contact with other people only after his fear disappears, then he can never break through his obsession. What he can do is face people regardless of his fear or nervousness. This is the reality of *arugamama*.

A girl had been told by a doctor that she should give in to her anxiety and wash her hands as often as she wanted. Under this kind of guidance her symptoms worsened to the point where she had to have her mother wipe her bottom after going to the toilet. This is not genuine *arugamama*.

Suppose a patient compulsively wipes his glasses at work because they have dust on them. In this case the obsession is the urge to wipe away the dust, and the compulsive action is to wipe. The impulse of wanting to wipe emerges as a reflex that has already become an irresistible, obsessive phenomenon. If he is going to quit only after this impulse fades away, he will never be freed from his compulsive behavior.

To bear an obsession is very hard. The easiest way to alleviate his immediate suffering is to behave compulsively, but such behavior does not solve anything. Even if he cannot prevent this obsession from appearing, there is still room to use his free will to control whether he acts on his obsession. When you are captured by such a symptom, you cannot do anything about the occurrence of the obsession of wanting to wipe the dust from your glasses, but you can resist taking the action of wiping if you bear the suffering and make an effort. Leaving the obsession as it is and, at the same time, ceasing to behave compulsively, then acting on a constructive desire to live a healthy life—this approach is the real *arugamama*.

Morita's "Desire to Live"

Now I would like to take up the issue of Morita's "desire to live" [*sei no yokubou*]. I understand the meaning of this desire to live as the desire to live better, the desire to improve and develop. We could debate the question of what is improvement and what is development, but for now please just accept it with your common sense. Affirming the desire to live expresses Morita's optimistic view of life.

This desire to live exists in human beings as a basic drive. The adaptation anxiety which I mentioned before is, so to speak, the opposite side of this desire. If there is no desire to live, then there is no adaptation anxiety. To try to improve and develop according to the desire to live is the way of *arugamama*. In the case of obsessional neurosis, *arugamama* means to leave the occurrence of obsession as it is, and, following the desire to improve and develop, make constructive efforts without obsessive behavior. This attitude is totally different from giving in to obsession.

A person with a fear of facing others should have contact with people while enduring his fear. A person with anxiety neurosis can nervously get on a train. A person who feels heaviness in his head can do whatever he can, even with the handicap of his symptoms. After having the experience of doing things while experiencing their symptoms, for the first time they can have confidence. The symptoms begin to lose their power, becoming ordinary occurrences which sometimes happen to mind and body.

The treatment of neurosis, especially obsessive neurosis, is very much like the practice of giving up smoking, so

I would like to talk about my experience of quitting smoking. I started smoking when I was a high school student and became a very heavy smoker. I stopped smoking ten years ago, and I have never smoked since. I had tried to stop before then. One of the reasons that I did not succeed was that the harm of smoking was not clear to me then. However, it became clearer that smoking is harmful for health. Statistics showed that it shortens the span of life. I also had bronchitis. So I decided to quit smoking. However, the power of several decades of habit was so strong that the impulse to smoke attacked me strongly, and I could not do anything about it. If I had waited to give up smoking until after this impulse went away, then I could never have stopped. I was supported by the desire to live, which meant that I wanted to keep my health. Having the desire to smoke and trying to endure it was a great pain, but as the days went by, gradually the pain disappeared. Eventually, continuing to avoid smoking even started to give me pleasure. Smoking and neurotic symptoms are different, but I think the psychological process of overcoming them must be similar.

In this connection I remember the story of Mr. Hyakuzo Kurata's (author: 1891–1943) experiences. One day I met Mr. Kurata at Dr. Morita's house and heard his story directly. He had days of facing blank writing paper, not being able to write any sentences, because of his strong obsession. We call it compulsive behavior when someone does something unnecessary because of obsession. Failing to do necessary things because of obsession is called obsessive prohibition. Mr. Kurata's obsessive prohibition lasted quite a long time, and his financial situation was becoming critical. Eventually he felt so desperate that he had nothing left to lose. Then he began writing. He found out that he could write. The work he did at that time was a short story called "Fuyu Hototogisu." He thought it was one of the best of his works. What he said deeply impressed me. He used the paradoxical expression "cured without being cured" because he could write despite his obsession. That is, leaving the obsession as it was (*arugamama*), he wrote from his fundamental desire to write and grow. That attitude is *arugamama*.

Morita Therapy: A Total Method of Treatment

We talk to the patients, as stated before, and we guide them in the practice of *arugamama*. We try to use therapeutic methods that cure physical and mental disorders by means of psychological processes, but that is not the entirety of Morita Therapy. It is often insufficient to merely clarify the pathology, help patients understand the treatment plan, and guide them in practicing it. It is sometimes necessary to conduct the inpatient treatment that Morita practiced.

We use a combination of clinical methods, which include an environmental change by hospitalization, the patient's absolute confinement in bed, physical work and games, communal living, journal guidance, dialogue, and so on.

Neurotic symptoms are responses to the environment, even though such reactions may be more or less indirect. It is well known that reactions to physical confinement improve just by transferring patients to freer environments. Although not that drastic, the change in environment by hospitalization helps free patients from the idleness that allows them to be selfish. Also, this new environment has both a warm, friendly, family-like atmosphere and the strictness of a hospital. Absolute confinement in bed means rest and recuperation. It also cuts off the psychic interaction of confronting suffering and worry. At the same time it is expected to have a psychological influence of increased boredom from inactivity, hunger for stimuli, and the building of a desire for activity.

Living in groups (usually from 10 to 20 members) encourages inpatients to socialize. Those who have felt they were unique can realize directly that there are many people who have the same kinds of symptoms. Group life helps them to be free from the sense of discrimination they have felt up to now, and they begin to acquire a perspective of equality. They make more effort, encouraged by the progress of others.

Keeping a daily journal in which a doctor writes comments deepens the relationship between the doctor and the patient. The doctor's comments help the patient to reflect on himself, and the journal helps the doctor to know the patient's condition better. The same can be said about the dialogues between doctor and patient.

Physical work and games free patients from their self-centered defensive attitudes by helping them become aware of the outside world and events happening around them. They can gain confidence in being able to keep active, even with their symptoms. It helps reduce the power of their symptoms. To live a healthy life means to be positively active in mind and body. A healthy lifestyle is the way to health, in mental health, too.

As mentioned above, the Morita way of clinical treatment is a total treatment approach that combines various methods to help eliminate patients' symptoms, increase their adaptability, and foster constructive attitudes toward life. Therefore, we can see that calling Morita Therapy merely a hospital confinement therapy, a work therapy or a diary therapy may invite misunderstanding. Each of these methods may be called psychiatric treatment in a broad sense, but individually they are too limited. Morita Therapy inpatient treatment consists of all these elements. They work together complementarily within the whole system.

Neurotic symptoms include obsessive fear of inter-personal contact, insomnia, heaviness in the head, fear of not completing something, and so on. If both patients and doctors look at the symptoms superficially they tend to try temporary measures of treatment. They draw the hasty conclusion that the purpose of treatment is achieved as long as the symptoms disappear. However, as I said in the beginning, the roots of the apparent symptoms lie far deeper, in the distorted personalities of patients. It is necessary to look at these roots in order to treat neurosis. Therefore, I believe that using only such methods as explanation, persuasion or suggestion is insufficient in more serious cases of neurosis.

Morita Therapy works on the whole personality, and it tries to increase adaptability and have patients practice constructive attitudes toward life. In addition to psychological procedures, it incorporates other methods that serve this purpose, too. I think this is one of the main characteristics of Morita Therapy.

At present psychiatric therapy is in the process of development. No method yet has effectiveness as great as the chemical treatment for tuberculosis, for example. How will psychiatric treatment develop from now on? I imagine that the most effective mental treatment must be one which incorporates and synthesizes the best of various treatment methods in a total system.

13

The Essence of Morita Therapy

Obsession and Freedom

I often see magazine articles about the experiences of people who were cured by Morita Therapy. However, I rarely see the publication of stories written by people whose neuroses were cured by other therapies. I believe that this is another characteristic of Morita Therapy that distinguishes it from other mental therapies; that is, people who are cured by Morita Therapy do not keep their experiences only to themselves. They want to share their experiences with as many people as possible. They hope that their stories will help or guide others. They cannot have this kind of desire while they are obsessed with their symptoms.

Yesterday I received a letter that was ten pages of small, closely written characters. It was from a female school teacher. Although her name and address were on an enclosed return envelope, the letter was not signed. She begged me to send a response, and she also strongly cautioned me not to tell anyone. If one is obsessed, that is the way one behaves.

A policeman whose fear of interpersonal contact was cured by hospitalization at Koseiin contributed the detailed story of his experience to a magazine called *Jikei*, which is published by the police department. There is a world of difference between the state of mind of that kind of person and one who does not want anyone else to know about him. I suppose many people who read this book have neurotic symptoms. I think that when you can announce them in public, that is the time when you are greatly relieved of your symptoms.

There are quite a few neurotics who think only about themselves. Once one of my patients cut his foot on a piece of glass in the garden when he was working in bare feet. He came into the dispensary for treatment. Of course, it was unfortunate that the broken glass was there in the first place, but I asked him, "What did you do with the pieces ?" He said he had left them there.

I said, "That's no good. You are only concerned about your own injury. If you leave them there, others may get hurt. Why don't you pick them up and throw them away?"

He had a skeptical look on his face, but he wrote in his journal, "Today I got injured; moreover, I was scolded by the doctor. But after long thought I realized that he was right." When a patient is only concerned about himself, his obsessions worsen. This is the distortion of self-defense.

The Desire to Live

I have often spoken and written about the essence of Morita Therapy, but I suppose good things should be planted in our minds repeatedly. There are not very many methods in the treatment of neurosis, so what is said all sounds just about the same. However, things discussed often become your own flesh and blood. You may say, "Not again!" but please bear with me and keep reading.

The first main point of Morita Therapy concerns the desire to live. The desire to live is not limited to human beings, but common to all living things. When I visited

Manazuru the last time, I went to a cactus park. Cactus plants grow where there is little humidity, so they have a mechanism to avoid dehydration as much as possible. The cactus gradually evolved to adapt to desert climates. To prevent dehydration it became a pole-like body by making its surface area as small as possible. Bodies that hold a lot of water tend to suffer from foreign invasions. So cacti have thorns. Although it is not conscious itself, it evolved that way because of the survival of the fittest.

Camels are fit to live in the desert, where there is no water, and so they have one or two humps. The humps hold a lot of fat that can become a source of energy and water. The camel's nostrils droop down so that the sand does not get into its nose during sandstorms. Its splayed feet keep it from being buried in the sand.

Like the cactus and the camel, plants and animals apply their ingenuity in various ways to live in their environments. Of course, such lower animals or plants do not consciously use their inventiveness to adapt themselves. They adapt naturally because of natural selection. The desire to live in human beings goes beyond such fundamental mechanisms, having progressed to a higher level; we want to live better and to prosper. That is the characteristic of the human desire to live.

A neurotic person has an especially strong desire to live. However, there is definitely a fear of death on the other side of this desire to live. These are the two sides of the coin. If there were no desire to live, there would be no fear of death. Therefore, some neurotic symptoms show the fear of death itself, and many symptoms are indirectly connected with the fear of death. The fear of illness is an obvious example, but if you interpret the fear of death in a broader sense, this applies to neurotic symptoms as a whole.

Sometimes one cannot adapt to the outside world in his present mental and physical condition, and he is afraid that he may be rejected by his society. To him that means the same as his death in a broad sense, for his social anxiety is connected with the fear of death. In this way people who have a strong desire to live usually have strong adaptation anxieties even if they are not conscious of their fear of death.

If we do not accept things as they are, and if we try to rid ourselves of them, then our minds tend to stay with them. That is why we become obsessed by them. A man could not help but listen to the sound of falling rain, so he got up in the middle of the night and put straw mats wherever raindrops fell. Another man could not stand dogs barking, and so he asked his father to drive them away with a stick every night. What an undutiful son! The stronger one wants to be rid of something, the more it sticks to him. Ordinary people do not pay much attention to such sounds. They usually accept them as they are. Of course, they may think it is a minor nuisance, but they accept it as it is because they can't do anything about it.

If people let go of things naturally, their attention does not stay in one place too long. It wanders away, so although the sound may still be there they do not hear it. That is our normal attitude. Even people who are obsessed by their symptoms have normal attitudes toward everything except the thing concerning their symptoms. They are not in any way different regarding other psychological or physiological matters.

When one tries to eliminate something that he thinks is blocking his desire to live, or tries to resist or rebel against it, the fight against this thing becomes his main purpose in life. Realistic, direct action to achieve his goal of living becomes paralyzed. Since human psychology cannot place importance on two things at the same time, if one strives to eliminate obstacles, then he neglects his efforts to satisfy his primary desire to live.

A person who fears relations with other people worries about what others think of him, or how his facial expressions appear, or whether he is blushing when he faces others. If he is acting upon his real desire to live, then he can get on with the business at hand, but instead he is enslaved by the opinions of others, and his mind focuses on himself. His main purpose becomes fighting against his psychological tendencies in order to eliminate them. He neglects the real purpose of dialogue, which is the topic or business matter at the time. When he is in the presence of others his mind is in chaos. I call this tendency "making the means into the objective."

In any case, he thinks of the means as his purpose. When he reads books, he thinks he should not have distracting thoughts because they get in his way. That is, his main purpose becomes the elimination of stray thoughts. That is why he is conscious of his random thoughts one by one. Ridding himself of his distracting thoughts, which should be a means, becomes a purpose, replacing the real purpose of reading. Cases of neurosis are usually like this.

No one likes illness, and so it is natural to fear it; however, for someone obsessed by hypochondria, avoiding illness becomes the greatest purpose of his life. Why does he think he shouldn't be ill? Because he can't exert his ability fully. Because of his desire to live, it is unsatisfactory to be ill, and, therefore, he shouldn't be ill. This is the natural psychology of the reverse side of wanting to live. One who does not catch diseases is not necessarily a superior human being. If that were the case, then perhaps pigs can be placed as higher animals than humans since they do not get food poisoning, regardless of what they eat.

Dr. Morita was sickly and mostly bedridden in his last year. Even then, in the times when he did not have a fever, he used to write. Despite the considerable effort he did his work according to his condition. When he had a little fever, he read. When he had a little more fever, he listened to someone else read. He did what he could do depending on his condition.

Shiki Masaoka (poet: 1867–1902) had a very serious illness. Spinal caries gave him sharp, nearly unbearable pain. In his last year he was bedridden. He could not even turn over in bed. In this condition he produced great work by dictating it to someone. If avoiding illness is the only purpose of human life, then Shiki Masaoka and Dr. Morita were insignificant people. Of course, the premise is false so the conclusion is false, too.

Constructive Efforts in the Course of Treatment

Regarding the course of treatment, you probably know the gist of it from what I have already mentioned. Neurosis arises from anxiety about being unable to adapt. This anxiety is the reverse of the desire to live. The more one tries to eliminate anxiety, the stronger it becomes. All efforts result in a reverse effect. There is no other way than simply to accept anxiety with humility.

Moreover, symptoms typically bend one's mental tendencies into one direction over a long period of time. Obsessive ideas appear every so often. A person who fears interpersonal contact experiences fear as a reflex before he actually meets someone. A person who has a fear of uncleanliness has a desire to wash his hands every time he sees certain objects. A person with anxiety neurosis suffers severe anxiety attacks every time he gets on a train. The symptoms of a neurotic person occur habitually, and they attack almost automatically.

The urge to smoke attacked me irresistibly when I renounced tobacco. We can assume that neurosis is the same kind of thing. Therefore, it is useless to try to resist it. Not only that, resisting yields the counter result of being more strongly obsessed. There is no other way than to simply accept it as it is. This is the first policy of treatment.

The next important point is the desire for growth and development. The symptoms occur as irresistible reflexes, so leave them as they are and strive according to your desire to grow. I often use the following example: Fear attacks inevitably when one tries to jump into a swimming pool from a high diving platform. One who does not have any fear is exceptional. If one avoids jumping in because of his fear, then he does not have a strong desire for development. He is one who gives up easily. One becomes a weak-willed person if he gives up too easily.

I often watch sumo wrestling on television. There are some wrestlers who quickly give up, and they quit fighting as soon as they are pushed. However, it is not good to hold on to the impossible either. For example, you can't change the past. However, it is worse to give up too quickly. If you give up everything too easily, then you become weak-willed.

A neurotic's problem is not that he leaves a job unfinished, but that his fear makes it difficult for him to act, and so he thinks everything will be all right as long as he eliminates the fear. Such becomes his reasoning. He thinks fear is in his way, and he wants to eliminate this obstacle. So with all his might he tries to overcome his fear. However, fear naturally accompanies the desire to live, so one cannot do anything about the fear which comes inevitably when he jumps into the water the first time from a high diving platform. Fear can't be resisted.

If one tries to avoid his fear, he gets into the dilemma of trying to do the impossible. If he is always concerned about his terror, always wonders why he has it, always grieves about it, he develops an inferiority complex, a querulous attitude. In his mind there is always conflict. Although he wants to improve, he still cannot rid himself of his fear, and that is a contradiction in reality. When the contradiction becomes acute, he becomes neurotic.

What about a healthy attitude? When one wants to jump into water, if he has such a desire for growth and development, then there is no alternative but to bear the fear. There is no other means but to jump in with his fear. He can do that. He can jump even though he cannot eliminate his fear.

One has a relatively wide latitude of action, however. A person who fears contact with other people should have a smiling expression in front of others according to his real wish to be liked. His desire is to avoid making a bad impression on others. I tell him, "When you see people smiling, you feel good, so why don't you smile at them?" But he insists, "When I feel bad because of my fear, there is no way I can smile."

Facial expressions are made by muscles we can control freely. That is why we can say, "cheese," when our pictures are taken in order to have smiling expressions. Therefore, even if you feel bad, or if you have a headache because of a slight cold, you can smile when someone comes to see you. You have freedom of action.

When you have obsessive thoughts, you cannot freely control the occurrence of the thoughts themselves, but if you endure them you can control unnecessary actions which normally accompany your obsessive ideas. You cannot do anything about the impulse to wash your hands, but you can endure it. Obsessive ideas arise uncontrollably, but you can control your attitude toward them and take constructive action. To do it you need endurance. All humans are made to bear pain to a certain degree; otherwise, we could not keep the right course.

There are quite a few things we have to bear in order to live. If we try, we surely can pursue constructive efforts in spite of wanting to take the easy way out.

To the Degree There Is Anxiety There Is Possibility

Neurotics can succeed in constructive actions if they try. They have strong desires for improvement, and their desire to live is strong. The result is that they rebel against obstacles and develop neuroses. One characteristic of neurotics is that they have innately strong desires to improve their lives.

Therefore, there are many who have overcome neurosis and who are well established in society. The former patients of Koseiin Hospital made a group called Keyakikai. Among them are presidents of large corporations, capable civil servants, engineers, and war veterans with many medals. Of course, rising up in the world is not the only purpose of life. Nevertheless, there are quite a few who can live well as full-fledged members of society because they have an innate capacity to do quite a lot if they try.

I always say to my patients, "Do you really want to get better and improve yourself? If not, you do not have to come here, and you do not have to listen to me. There is no need for you to try. Think seriously." Then they tell me they want to make a decent living, but they are obsessed by the idea that they have to do something about the obstacles which block the achievement of their goals. Nevertheless, their real desire is to improve a great deal, and they want to exercise their abilities.

Please consider carefully whether you really have the desire to live or not. Then you will surely recognize that you have such a desire to utilize your abilities fully. People who have neuroses have such desires; they are not innately weak-willed, nor can they become worthless.

They cannot be satisfied living as weak-willed people. Therefore, if they continue life without constructive work because of their neurotic symptoms, they begin to dislike themselves. They do not like themselves because they are leading dissatisfying lives that do not meet their real wishes. If they are living in ways that satisfy their true needs, then they can feel delightful joy, even with painful or distressing experiences.

People with neurotic symptoms, especially those with obsessive behavior, can live constructive lives, even with their symptoms. They can live happily. They can believe in themselves and have confidence.

Dr. Morita frequently used to talk about the desire to live. Unlike Freud, Dr. Morita was basically an optimist who believed in the growth and development of human beings. Freud said that humans are wolves to other humans. He even wrote of the death wish. He could not optimistically trust the progress and development of human society. He strongly believed that instinct was very cruel. Dr. Morita's basic theory is that people wish to live, and moreover, he affirmed the desire to live constructively in his work. He was fundamentally optimistic.

Dr. Morita's doctrine is based on believing in the desire to live, the desire for growth and development. This means that you can grow and develop. I can assure you beyond doubt that you can become a useful person in society if you master Dr. Morita's theory and put it into practice.

When you are young, your past is short and your future is very long. You may not have done many things in the recent past, so you have not been able to recognize your own capabilities accurately. You have not yet done much. When you have done many things, you unexpectedly discover things that you can do, but you cannot really trust your abilities when you have done little. That is why you have a lot of uncertainty in your future. Given your short record of past performance, no one can guarantee that you will be able to cope with your long future.

When one becomes my age, he has done just about everything he can do. Sumo wrestlers often retire after they reach thirty, saying they have done enough and that there is nothing more to do. My state of mind is something like theirs. I know my abilities more or less. I know it is not much more than what I can see now, so I am at ease. However, I cannot expect that much development in my future, so I am forlorn in that sense. When one is young, he has great anxiety about his future, but that future is attractive. Where there is no anxiety there is not much appeal. Young people experience a lot of anxiety about the future, but great possibilities lie there. The future is very appealing.

I sincerely hope that you will make your best efforts with your understanding of the principal ideas of neurotic treatment.

Index